THE END AND THE MYTH

THE END AND THE MYTH

By the Editors of

TIME-LIFE BOOKS

with text by

Paul O'Neil

TIME-LIFE BOOKS / ALEXANDRIA, VIRGINIA

Time-Life Books Inc.
is a wholly owned subsidiary of

TIME INCORPORATED

Founder: Henry R. Luce 1898-1967

Editor-in-Chief: Henry Anatole Grunwald
Chairman of the Board: Andrew Heiskell
President: James R. Shepley
Editorial Director: Ralph Graves
Vice Chairman: Arthur Temple

TIME-LIFE BOOKS INC.

Managing Editor: Jerry Korn
Executive Editor: David Maness
Assistant Managing Editors: Dale M. Brown
(planning), George Constable, George G. Daniels
(acting), Martin Mann, John Paul Porter
Art Director: Tom Suzuki
Chief of Research: David L. Harrison
Director of Photography: Robert G. Mason
Senior Text Editor: Diana Hirsh
Assistant Art Director: Arnold C. Holeywell
Assistant Chief of Research: Carolyn L. Sackett
Assistant Director of Photography: Dolores A. Littles

Chairman: Joan D. Manley
President: John D. McSweeney
Executive Vice Presidents: Carl G. Jaeger,
John Steven Maxwell, David J. Walsh
Vice Presidents: Nicholas Benton (public relations),
Nicholas J. C. Ingleton (Asia), James L. Mercer
(Europe/South Pacific), Herbert Sorkin
(production), Paul R. Stewart (marketing),
Peter G. Barnes, John L. Canova
Personnel Director: Beatrice T. Dobie
Consumer Affairs Director: Carol Flaumenhaft
Comptroller: George Artandi

THE OLD WEST

EDITORIAL STAFF FOR "THE END AND THE MYTH"
Editor: Jim Hicks
Picture Editor: Richard Kenin
Text Editors: David Johnson, John Manners,
Lydia Preston
Designer: Edward Frank
Staff Writers: Russell B. Adams Jr., Paul Clancy,
Mark M. Steele
Chief Researcher: Carol Forsyth Mickey
Researchers: Michael Blumenthal, Feroline Burrage,
Mindy A. Daniels, Barbara Fleming, Ann Kuhns,
Sara Mark, Heather Mason Sandifer, Nancy Toff,
Betty H. Weatherley
Art Assistant: Van W. Carney
Editorial Assistant: Barbara Brownell

EDITORIAL PRODUCTION
Production Editor: Douglas B. Graham
Operations Manager: Gennaro C. Esposito,
Gordon E. Buck (assistant)
Assistant Production Editor: Feliciano Madrid
Quality Control: Robert L. Young (director),
James J. Cox (assistant), Daniel J. McSweeney,
Michael G. Wight (associates)
Art Coordinator: Anne B. Landry
Copy Staff: Susan B. Galloway (chief),
Elise Ritter Gibson, Celia Beattie
Picture Department: Linda Hensel

THE AUTHOR: Paul O'Neil's knowledge of the West is firsthand and intimate. The grandson of a California gold prospector, he grew up in Seattle and worked there as short-story writer and news-paperman (in the late 1930's, one of the last surviving frontier marshals demonstrated his fast draw for reporter O'Neil, an event the author recounts in Chapter One of this book). Later, as a staff writer for TIME, SPORTS ILLUSTRATED and LIFE, O'Neil often wrote about Western characters, from rodeo cowboys to Texas oil wildcatters. His previous volumes in the Old West series were *The Rivermen* and *The Frontiersmen*.

THE COVER: Playing the legendary Old West hero Wild Bill Hickok, actor William S. Hart brandishes his six-guns in a 1923 movie poster. Hart's portrayals of Western characters in silent films helped to keep the frontier myth—and some of the frontier reality—alive in the minds of 20th Century Americans. The frontispiece: Jim Eskew Jr., a 1940s trick-roping champion, leaps through his twirling lariat from atop his horse. Eskew performed in rodeos, which—like films—exploited and at the same time preserved aspects of the 19th Century West.

CORRESPONDENTS: Elisabeth Kraemer (Bonn); Margot Hapgood, Dorothy Bacon, Lesley Coleman (London); Susan Jonas, Lucy T. Voulgaris (New York); Maria Vincenza Aloisi, Josephine du Brusle (Paris); Ann Natanson (Rome). Valuable assistance was also provided by: Karen Hills (Copenhagen); Naomi Narod, Penny Newman (London); Diane Asselin (Los Angeles); Carolyn T. Chubet, Miriam Hsia, Christina Lieberman (New York); Mimi Murphy (Rome); Janet Zich (San Francisco).

For information about any Time-Life book, please write:
Reader Information
Time-Life Books
541 North Fairbanks Court
Chicago, Illinois 60611

Library of Congress Cataloguing in Publication Data
Time-Life Books.
　The End and The Myth.
　(The Old West; 26)
　Bibliography: p.
　Includes index.
　1. The West—History—Miscellanea. 2. Frontier and pioneer life
—The West—Miscellanea. 3. Western films—History and criticism.
4. The West in literature—History and criticism.
I. O'Neil, Paul, 1909-　　II. Title.
III. Series: The Old West (Alexandria, Va.); 26.
F591.T57 1979　　978　　78-26389
ISBN 0-8094-2314-6
ISBN 0-8094-2313-8 lib. bdg.

Other Publications:

THE EPIC OF FLIGHT
THE GOOD COOK
THE SEAFARERS
THE ENCYCLOPEDIA OF COLLECTIBLES
THE GREAT CITIES
WORLD WAR II
HOME REPAIR AND IMPROVEMENT
THE WORLD'S WILD PLACES
THE TIME-LIFE LIBRARY OF BOATING
HUMAN BEHAVIOR
THE ART OF SEWING
THE EMERGENCE OF MAN
THE AMERICAN WILDERNESS
THE TIME-LIFE ENCYCLOPEDIA OF GARDENING
LIFE LIBRARY OF PHOTOGRAPHY
THIS FABULOUS CENTURY
FOODS OF THE WORLD
TIME-LIFE LIBRARY OF AMERICA
TIME-LIFE LIBRARY OF ART
GREAT AGES OF MAN
LIFE SCIENCE LIBRARY
THE LIFE HISTORY OF THE UNITED STATES
TIME READING PROGRAM
LIFE NATURE LIBRARY
LIFE WORLD LIBRARY
FAMILY LIBRARY:
　HOW THINGS WORK IN YOUR HOME
　THE TIME-LIFE BOOK OF THE FAMILY CAR
　THE TIME-LIFE FAMILY LEGAL GUIDE
　THE TIME-LIFE BOOK OF FAMILY FINANCE

CONTENTS

1 | Farewell to a fabled era

From the time the country was founded, Americans had seen the West as a virtually inexhaustible repository of new living space. Always, just one bound beyond the fringe of civilization, there was room to stretch for a better life, with good, rich earth free to anyone who was sufficiently daring and hard-working to claim it and use it.

In the early 19th Century, national leaders predicted it would take 500 years to populate the vast West. But by the 1890s, America's headiest era of expansion was over. Rail lines crosshatched the prairie, and farms and towns flourished where Indians had hunted buffalo a few decades earlier.

The passing of what came to be called the Old West was marked most tangibly by the arrival of modern technology. Advances in agricultural machinery enabled farmers to earn a living on land that had defied profitable cultivation. Telephones and automobiles made Western rural life less isolated. And as early as 1911, when a flight pioneer showed that coyotes could be hunted from an airplane, ranchers foresaw that stock on remote sections of their land could be inspected from the skies. Even the cowboy on horseback—the very symbol of the American West—would finally be outmoded as the guardian of the range.

A lone Wyoming cowboy looks over his shoulder at a plane scouting strays in the '30s.

7

8

Coloradans bring their traditional animal-drawn work vehicles together with a new steam tractor and power thresher for a photograph during a turn-of-the-century harvest. By 1890, new farm technology had reduced to three man-hours the labor necessary to produce an acre of wheat—down from 61 hours only a quarter of a century before.

San Diego's Electric Rapid Transit, the first trolley on the West Coast when it began service in 1887, stops near the end of the line to let off a passenger. The streetcar was but one indication that San Diego was leaving its old frontier ways behind: it already had electricity and the telephone.

While his horse—not suspecting the implications for the future of its kind—stands patiently by, a Wyoming cowboy greets automobile-delivered mail in 1931. By 1940, the number of working horses in the country had dropped to 10 million from 20 million just three decades before.

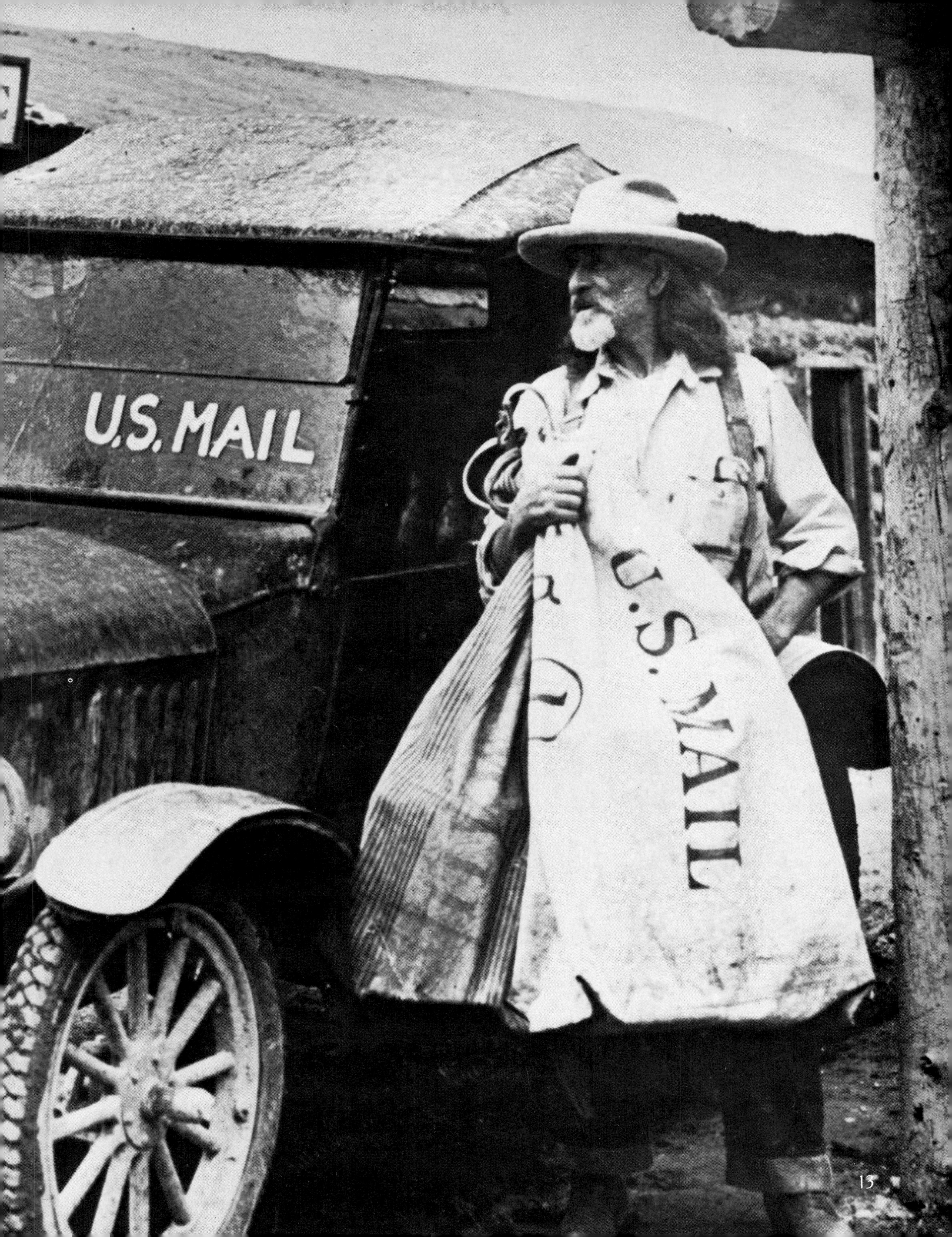
U.S. MAIL
U.S. MAIL

The lingering aura of a vanishing frontier

The Old West was long gone into history—dotted with cities, invaded by Packards, Overlands, Willys-Knights and the ubiquitous Model T, and as devoted to Stacomb and step-ins as Newark or Easthampton—when the Great Northern Railroad began driving an eight-mile tunnel through Washington state's Cascade Range in 1926. But the little town of Leavenworth, on the eastern slopes of the mountains, began behaving like Abilene or Dodge City, for all that, as cardsharps, whores, con men and bootleggers converged on the railroad's crews of laborers and hard-rock miners. The town coped with this dilemma in the old-fashioned way, conferring a marshal's star on Noble L. ("Dude") Brown, a lean, quiet fellow with pale blue eyes and an ascetic devotion to the punctilio of the fast draw.

Dude Brown proved the wisdom of this regression in law enforcement after a gang of armed troublemakers exacerbated differences between construction labor groups by hunting for enemies along the main street during one dark night and leaving a backwash of apprehensive citizens in its wake. The offenders had disappeared by the time the lawman—"I always walked in smiling"—arrived at the scene of their displeasure. "But I knew where they'd gone," Brown recalled years afterward. "There was an abandoned railroad station down the tracks and they was there waiting for a freight to get out of town."

Brown walked alone through the darkness along the railroad line and into the gaping doorway of the old building. "They had a candle burning in there—stuck on the floor—and they was all sitting around it in a half

"Dude" Brown, who carried the tradition of the frontier lawman into the '20s as marshal of Leavenworth, Washington, was called "one of the last links with the Old West" when he died in 1942.

circle. They had guns, of course, some of them. I said, 'Any of you boys packing a wagon? Lay them down on the floor.' None of them said anything. One of them with a pistol got up and walked around behind me. I never turned. I looked at them in front of me. I knew I'd be able to see in their eyes if he drawed and I knew I could kill him and a couple more of them, too, before they got me. They knowed it too. The one behind me walked back in a couple of minutes and dropped his gun. I said, 'One at a time,' and the rest did the same. Then we all walked back to the jail."

The tunnel was completed in 1929. Leavenworth resumed its quiet ways. Brown became a county commissioner and later a member of the state legislature, and took to wearing a business suit. But he did not abandon the instincts and attitudes of his youth. He had been a broncobuster and cowhand at 14, and had developed his deadly artistry with a pistol in gunfights with rustlers who drifted along the border in the empty Okanogan country looking for cattle to run into Canada. He clung to a simple philosophy: "Never double cross a man. Never back down." And he buckled on belt, holster and revolver daily to practice the draw. He was secretive about this preoccupation—he had a sense of reserve and propriety—but once reluctantly consented to demonstrate his skill for a reporter who was curious about a rite so dramatically embedded in American folklore.

Brown took off his jacket, buckled on the gun belt and, in the course of doing so, changed in some indefinable and curiously menacing way. He stared dispassionately at his visitor, and the gun was magically in his hand. His fingers had closed, his wrist had turned—but how, in a split second, had the weapon cleared its leather container? Would he do it once more? He said nothing. He slid the gun home, was still, arms down, for a few seconds—and then stood holding the pistol

A LAST HURRAH FOR THE DEADWOOD COACH

As railroads spread across the West, stagecoaches rolled away into their final sunset. When the last Northwestern coach left Deadwood, South Dakota, on December 28, 1890, the town turned out to bid farewell. Cheering citizens in top hats, led by the Deadwood band, saw the coach off on its final run to Rapid City, where this picture was taken. Deadwood eagerly awaited the railroad—which began service the following day—but even so the merriment was tinged with sadness. Opined a local columnist: "The railroad has come, though in our rejoicing we remember the departure of an old pleasant sight that has whirled through our streets these many long years."

aimed at his guest's belly. He unbuckled the belt, hesitated, and said with a kind of awkward modesty—and as if the year were 1880 rather than 1936: "Well, you see, I've got an edge. I wouldn't want you to spread this . . . the wrong man might hear about it. But," voice dropping a little, "look here. I sprinkle talcum powder in the holster."

The West was embracing technology of a thousand different varieties as he spoke. The Boeing Aircraft Company was building transport planes just over the mountains in Seattle. Corporate geologists had replaced the lone prospector. Cowboys had begun tending cattle in pickup trucks. The Indian had long since been incarcerated on reservations, and the land had long since been divided up from territories into states.

The Old West as a definable era had ended, and yet here stood Dude Brown as living, breathing evidence that some part of it somehow lived on.

The Old West had not vanished overnight. Frontier life was already altering when the Appalachian backwoodsmen first spilled into Kentucky and Tennessee with axes, long rifles and whiskey stills, and evolution's inexorable progress had been isolating Westerners like Brown—custodians of waning attitudes and obsolescent skills—for a century before his own day.

Mountain men who roamed the Rockies to trap beaver in the early 19th Century gathered for a last rendezvous—their annual whoop-up and fur-trading session—in 1840. Most of them then turned to other professions, outmoded by a falling demand for beaver pelts and depletion of the animals themselves. Pony Express riders who thundered into legend while speeding mail cross-country lost their moment of glory in 1861 when telegraph wires made their service obsolete. Scouts who led the early settlers' wagon trains through the wilderness were being replaced before the Civil War by maps, guidebooks and well-marked trails.

The pace of change accelerated as the century aged. Professional buffalo hunters outmoded themselves in the early 1880s—and sealed the fate of the Plains Indians—by killing off all but a few remnants of the country's bison, which only two decades before had numbered 13 million. The hunters were followed by a curious army of scavengers who moved in behind them

No home on the range: a bison herd's journey into exile

By the turn of the century, the buffalo was almost homeless in the American West. Congress had prohibited the killing of bison in 1894, but provided only two small sanctuaries that could hold a mere 65 animals. The lawmakers ignored the plight of private breeders, who owned most of the nation's bison but were unable to maintain their expanding herds without government land grants.

In 1906, when legislators refused to buy and shelter the nation's largest herd, its angry owner—a part Indian named Michel Pablo—sold his stock to the Canadian government, which was creating a refuge in Alberta. Pablo spent the next four summers rounding up his 709 bison from their Montana range for shipment north. Each year the herd got more wary and feisty and it took 75 cowboys

two months to round up the last of the obstinate beasts *(below)* and move them 26 miles to the railroad loading corral.

In 1909, chagrined at losing the herd to Canada, Congress at last set aside 18,540 acres in Montana for a national bison range—too late to save Pablo's buffalo, but in time to establish a permanent and sizable herd as part of the nation's heritage.

Cowboys round up the last of Michel Pablo's buffalo herd *(left)* for the drive to the railroad stockyard at Ravalli, Montana *(right)*.

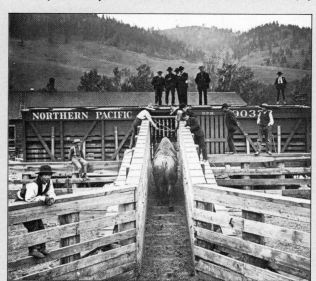 

One docile buffalo is prodded up to the cattle car *(left)*; however, a more spirited beast breaks its neck attempting to escape *(right)*.

to batten on their labors—and to hasten that erosion of the Old West that the hunters had helped to induce by eliminating its greatest wild herds. The buffalo killers left the prairies littered with bleaching bones, and railroads profited for years, as they advanced to continue the transformation of the frontier, by hauling tons of these skeletal remains to Eastern processing plants, which made them into carbon and fertilizers.

The era of open cattle ranges and of feudal cattle kings ended even faster than had the era of buffalo hunting. It lasted a mere 20 years after the Civil War, not only because of encroachment by settlers and unrealistic financing, but because its beef barons overgrazed their huge domains more recklessly each year.

Nutritious grasses covered the West's prairies and high plains before intrusion by stockmen—tall grasses that reached a man's chest, short grasses like gramma, bunch grass, buffalo grass and bluestem, and innumerable lesser ones with names like pleurisy root, sand dropseed and bluejoint turkeyfoot.

Few early cattlemen knew that this forage—rather than beef—constituted the grazing country's true wealth. There were 8.5 million cattle in Texas, more than two million in Kansas and more than a million each in Montana, New Mexico and Colorado by 1886 and the failing ground cover was attacked by millions of intruding sheep. Plant life was damaged almost beyond recovery and the beef bonanza collapsed in tangles of bankruptcies and dead cattle after awful blizzards in 1886-1887. Ranching survived, but as a prudent modern business conducted behind barbed wire, a fairly cheap fencing material first mass-produced in 1876. The railroads, meanwhile, spread their iron avenues into far reaches of cattle country, eliminating long trail drives as fences eliminated big roundups. The golden age of the cowboy was over.

The golden age of the West's Indians had ended long before, when white invaders first disrupted their traditional way of life; now their long, spirited fight to save some semblance of freedom came to an agonizing close. Resistance in the Southwest crumpled in 1886, when the Apache chieftain Geronimo was shipped off to prison in Florida. The northern Plains tribes, crippled by the destruction of the buffalo, yielded gradually to white force in the same period. The Battle of Wounded Knee in 1890 marked the close of the Indian wars. And the cessation of Indian hostilities was the beginning of the end for another Old West figure: the cavalry soldier. Many forts that once had dotted Western maps were abandoned; by 1897 only seven states or territories had more than two army posts.

White settlers poured into the West in ever larger numbers during the last quarter of the century, many of them traveling by rail (with the completion of the Great Northern Railroad in 1893 five rail links spanned the continent). They brought with them new techniques and new equipment—irrigation, modern plows, steam-powered harvesters and threshers—that made farming possible on the semiarid plains. New towns sprang up to serve the new farmers as marketing centers. A witness described this surging tide of settlement: "You may stand ankle deep in the short grass of the uninhabited wilderness; next month a train will glide over the waste and stop at some point where the railroad has decided to locate a town. Men, women and children will jump out, and their chattels will tumble out after them. From that moment the building begins."

It is possible to say this rapid settlement brought the Old West to an end, in the arbitrary statistical sense, around 1890. There had always been a line—recorded by succeeding generations of census takers, and still present after the 1880 census—beyond which the population dwindled in the West to less than two persons per square mile. But a compendium of the census of 1890 stated: "At present the unsettled area has been so broken by isolated bodies of settlements that there can hardly be said to be a frontier line." There were still great areas of open country, however, and the attitudes, pursuits and living conditions of the early West died hard in these empty fastnesses even though population was thickening on their flanks and big cities had long since risen on the Pacific Coast.

Dude Brown's Leavenworth thus was not the only town in which Western frontier practices survived the passing of the frontier. Vestiges of the earlier age lived on, not only because farmers, merchants, lawyers and teachers advanced into the wilderness at an uneven rate, but because they were influenced, on arrival, by the customs of the ranchers, cowhands, prospectors and saloonkeepers they gradually engulfed.

Men achieved prominence in the changing West of the early 20th Century as they had in the West of the

19th—because of character, daring or personal exploits. A wealthy man might be celebrated, but for the means by which he got his money or the way he used it rather than for its mere possession. Every man was conceded to be as good as his fellows until proved otherwise. Those who put on airs risked derision. This social abnegation stemmed from every man's hope of striking it rich tomorrow, from public acceptance of this wistful possibility, from the leveling influences of past hardships, and from a belief in the efficacy of physical rather than intellectual competence.

Die-hard inhabitants of remote areas—among them Sheriff Francis Joseph Wattron of Navajo County, Arizona Territory—staved off the end by ignoring outsiders bent on taming the West whenever possible and by giving them sardonic lip service when forced by circumstance to recognize the new order. Sheriff Wattron spent most of his time running a bar and drugstore while his deputy enforced the statutes, but he kept himself in the public eye by wearing a diamond-studded golden badge and by presiding at hangings. He outdid himself, however, with the notice for one execution:

"You are hereby invited to attend the hanging of one George Smiley, Murderer. His soul will be swung into eternity on December 8, 1899 at 2 o'clock P.M. sharp. The latest methods in the art of scientific strangulation will be done to make the surroundings cheerful and the execution a success."

The printer of the invitation leaked its text to an Albuquerque, New Mexico, newspaper, from which it was picked up by other publications. Prominent Easterners and Europeans were soon expressing their outrage. President McKinley himself reprimanded the governor of Arizona Territory, who admonished the sheriff in turn and ordered him to stay the proceedings until the public mind was diverted by other events. Wattron was taken aback—but fully equal to the occasion. This second invitation followed the first:

"Revised Statutes of Arizona, Penal Code, Title X, Section 1849, Page 807, makes it obligatory upon Sheriff to issue invitations to executions, form (unfortunately) not prescribed. With feelings of profound sorrow and regret, I hereby invite you to attend the private, decent and humane execution of a human being; name George Smiley; crime, murder. The said George Smiley will be executed on January 8, 1900 at

2 o'clock P.M. You are expected to deport yourself in a respectful manner and any 'flippant' or 'unseemly' language will not be allowed. Conduct tending to mar the solemnity of the occasion will not be tolerated."

Arizona—which did not become a state until 1912—was still wild and largely empty for years after Wattron's day. It organized a mounted police force, patterned after the Texas Rangers, in 1901. New Mexico followed in 1905 and Nevada as late as 1908. Arizona's Rangers, as described in an official publication, were "fearless men, trained in riding, roping, trailing and shooting," who came, "for the most part, from the interior of the Territory where they can be detailed with assurances of success owing to their knowledge of the country." And the West still had work for such men. A New Mexico deputy sheriff made this clear in a letter describing local conditions in a place called San Rafael. "The different factions are fighting one another and the place is in a turmoil with people shooting up the town and fighting all the time."

Such incidents dramatized the ephemeral nature of the Old West, for the attitudes they reflected could only have been temporary in a nation so devoted, in its entirety, to the rule of law. But they also dramatized

The posh resort of Manitou, Colorado, pictured here around 1900, offered healthful mineral baths to its wealthy patrons. Sniffed one guidebook, "Manitou is frequented by the *elite* of the territory, eastern *parvenus* and ailing invalids."

the Old West's instinct for survival, its complexity, the uneven nature of the processes that altered it in the end, and the difficulty of deciding, even today, just when the great American pilgrimage into its plains and mountains became an exercise in the commonplace—having played so definitive a role in the nation's history and dreams—and vanished forever into myth and memory.

The West was hardly settled before a feverish quest for petroleum inspired a kind of replay of the old days. Well into the 1930s the wildcatters of Texas, Oklahoma, Wyoming and California gambled for fortunes that dwarfed those of the Western gold stampedes and created boomtowns that were fully as crude, noisy and

dangerous as any that existed in the high plains and mountains during the 19th Century.

And the Wild West of myth—that product of romantics, liars, posturing *pistoleros* and writers of dime novels—coexisted from the beginning with the more mundane West of those sweat-stained fellows who actually branded cattle, sought pay dirt and garrisoned isolated forts on the upper Missouri.

The East had its way with the West from the start as well—not only by financing cattle ranches and mines, but as the supplier of items that tempted the pioneer's appetite for luxury and disturbed the purity of his surroundings. The narrator of Owen Wister's turn-of-the-century bestseller, *The Virginian,* finds the

Glossy ads from a cowpoke artist

At the turn of the century a prolific group of artists worked feverishly to document the disappearing frontier. One of the most popular was a Californian named Edward Borein, a onetime itinerant ranch hand who called himself the "Cowpuncher Artist."

Despite his lack of formal training, Borein was a talented and sought-after artist. He lived in New York to be close to the publishing offices where he peddled his work, but his Manhattan studio was crammed with saddles, guns, ropes and Indian artifacts to help him achieve authenticity. His pictures filled popular periodicals and appeared in advertisements to lend commercially valuable frontier appeal to such products as Pierce Arrow cars and Aunt Jemima pancakes. Borein's output of cowboy imagery continued until he died in 1945. He was the last major artist who, in the tradition of his better-known contemporaries Charles Russell and Frederic Remington, had ridden the range and known the Old West.

Borein painted the Old West eying the new in a 1911 ad.

prairie air "pure as water and strong as wine" but is bound to report the hero's lust for canned tomatoes and sardines, and describes the "ramparts" of Medicine Bow: "thick heaps and fringes of tin cans and shelving mounds of bottles cast out of the saloons."

There was always, in fact, a kind of Easterner's West encapsulated in the Westerner's West; globetrotting Britishers and adventurous swells from Boston and New York were out there among the Sioux and the buffalo with gun in hand almost as soon as Lewis and Clark got back from the Rockies. Author Wister, a Philadelphian, and the artist Frederic Remington, a New Yorker, later provided Westerners with a dramatic image they were unable to provide themselves, and Teddy Roosevelt—as amateur rancher, creator of the four-volume history *The Winning of the West,* and commander of the Rough Riders—created a breed of hard, enduring, brave and patriotic plainsmen all his own and advertised them (and, by implication, himself) as the very bone and marrow of triumphant America. And there was a posh Dude's West almost as soon as there were cowboys for the dudes to inspect.

Grand caravansaries like the Hotel de Paris in Georgetown, Colorado, and the hotels at Manitou near Colorado Springs began springing up in the early 1870s as the increasing lavishness of Pullman cars—which began boasting stained glass and thick carpeting—prompted the wealthy of Philadelphia, Boston and New York to take excursions into the far, empty reaches of the country. The Pullman, as noted by Lord Charles Russell on an American visit, "enabled the rich to create the clearest possible inequality in the conditions of even ordinary travel." Some Easterners, like Ralph Waldo Emerson on a Western adventure, rented private Pullmans, and wealthy families sometimes brought retinues of cooks, maids, nurses, porters and, as bodyguards, Pinkerton detectives.

They were not always entranced by the scenery. Ernest Ingersoll, author of *Knocking Round the Rockies,* described Arizona as "one of the very worst portions of the United States . . . repulsive plains of dry and thirsty sand, whose dreary waste is diversified by jagged buttes." But at an oasis like Manitou, Colorado, or the nearby Cheyenne Mountain Country Club, the wealthy adventurers were able to savor the wilderness while cocooned in luxury. "The ladies' breakfast toilets," wrote a visiting Englishman named Daniel Pidgeon, "are good enough for the dinner table, while for dinner they dress as we do for the opera. American ladies never walk but go out buggy riding in dancing shoes or amble about on ponies in highly ornamental riding habits." The gentlemen wore the latest in sporting fashions, too, while playing polo or riding to hounds (after coyotes).

But the West—in this case all the country between the Mississippi and the Pacific—was more, in the minds of Eastern industrialists and politicians, than a seat of cattle ranches, a kind of scrap heap for doleful Indians or a playground for eccentrics seeking vacations more exotic than those in Newport or Cape Cod. The West was seen as an enormous "safety valve" against social, industrial and political unrest. Jobless or recalcitrant laborers posed no real danger to the established order—or so the theory went—and a steady expansion of business was possible as long as the West had cheap, virgin land for the lower classes and exploitable resources for their betters. So much for the prophets of prosperity; prophets of doom materialized soon enough as it became apparent, when two depressions gripped the country's economy in the last quarter of the 19th Century, that cheap farming lands were on the verge of exhaustion out yonder.

The United States, according to many economists, would soon be forced to abandon the kind of prosperity it had accepted as its birthright for so long. This fear inspired demands—by thoughtful men as well as by bigots and crackpots—that immigration be closed, particularly against newly arriving contingents of Jews, Hungarians, Italians and other Eastern and Southern Europeans. Where would these "dregs" of the Continent go? What mischief might they not wreak if they could not be ushered off into the sagebrush? Such "alien breeds" would endanger the nation, said the president of the American Economics Association, when the West could no longer absorb them.

These dire views of the American future proved illusory in the long run, but they inspired endless magazine and newspaper articles and focused public attention on the West as it had not been focused since Custer's defeat. And they paved the way for an illumination of the frontier's place in national development— by an unknown young professor from Wisconsin, Frederick Jackson Turner—that has been a powerful influence on how Americans view the Old West, and how Americans view themselves, ever since. Turner's frontier thesis—delivered to a convocation of historians in Chicago on July 12, 1893—maintained that the beckoning wildernesses of the West, rather than the cultural legacies of Europe, had been the most important single influence in the formation of those concepts and customs that made the republic unique.

Turner's name means nothing to most Americans today, but he inspired a great many attitudes that millions of us still cherish, if only in our subconscious minds: that there is a bit of Kit Carson or Jim Bridger or Zebulon Pike (or even John Wayne) in all of us; that we became an unusual people in the country beyond the Appalachians—more resilient, more forthright, more adventurous and more self-reliant than those of races denied testing in the Rockies or on the Great Plains. Turner sanctified the West of myth, though he had no intention of doing so, by giving it thunderous new significance as he told his countrymen:

"To the frontier the American intellect owes its striking characteristics. That coarseness and strength combined with acuteness and inquisitiveness; that practical, inventive turn of mind, quick to find expedients; that masterful grasp of material things, lacking in the artistic but powerful to effect great ends; that restless, nervous energy; that dominant individualism working for good and for evil, and withal that buoyancy and exuberance which comes with freedom—these are traits of the frontier." Before Turner's time most of the country's historians were anchored in Eastern universities and were firmly convinced that little of importance occurred beyond the Appalachians. They believed that American attitudes and American institutions were almost wholly European imports.

This view of American politics and the American mind would inevitably have been altered. "The ideas underlying my 'Significance of the Frontier' would have been expressed in some form or other in any case," Turner acknowledged. "They were part of the growing American consciousness of itself." But Turner, a child of fortune if one ever lived, was moved to revolt against the established theory at exactly the right time. He captured the imagination of his countrymen at a moment in which they were ready to listen and thus made

A furniture manufacturer from Oregon sits with his wife and his son in cautious comfort amid a bristling collection of deer-horn pieces.

Frontier baroque in Western parlors

Westerners of the late 1800s were fully aware of the dime-novel stereotype they conjured in the imaginations of their countrymen back East. Many Westerners themselves found the image congenial and emulated the dress and manners of pulp heroes; local manufacturers responded by exaggerating the supposed Westernness of products like clothing and weapons. Even furniture makers began embellishing traditionally utilitarian decor by turning out elaborate creations of deer and cattle horn.

Where once a set of antlers had made a handy bunkhouse coat hook, now horns were fashioned into extravagantly ornate—and sometimes hazardous—adornments for opulent Western parlors. The table and hat rack at right, each priced at more than $200 in 1889, were made by a San Antonio manufacturer who assured customers that his materials came solely from Texas longhorn cattle. The rocking chair and foot stool were made in Oklahoma from the horns of steers the craftsman said he had killed himself.

LONGHORN TABLE

STEER-HORN ROCKING CHAIR

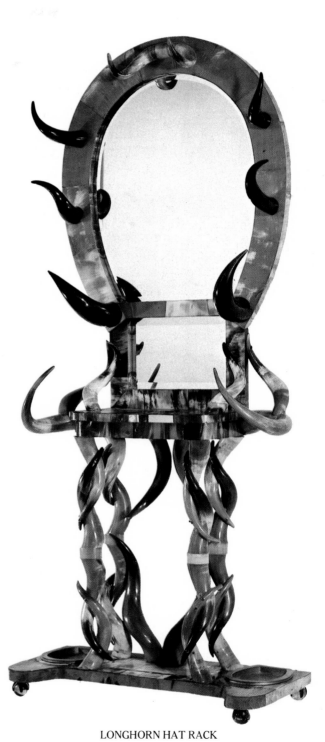

LONGHORN HAT RACK

STEER-HORN FOOT STOOL

himself the most influential of American historians.

He was a serious scholar with a scientific approach, but his frontier thesis seems to have been based at least in part on instinct and memories of boyhood. Turner was lucky in his birthplace, Portage, Wisconsin. The town was still on the edge of wilderness when Turner, who was born in 1861, was a schoolboy. Immigrant wagons rolled through on the way to the Dakotas, log drives came down the Wisconsin River from the northern pineries, and Indians shared the countryside until soldiers rounded them up and chased them farther west in the 1870s. There was occasional violence: two Irishmen fought a gun battle on the main street—and a mob hanged the winner for his pains.

But Portage offered the historian-to-be more prosaic evidence of the West's part in shaping American society, and particularly the part played by those backwoodsmen, farmers and merchants who succeeded the restless trapper, explorer and Indian trader. One third of the town's population was foreign-born—mainly Scotsmen, Welshmen and Germans—and many of the rest were fresh from other parts of the United States. They made up a "composite" people, who were "English in neither nationality nor characteristics," as he was to say later in describing "the rapid Americanization" worked by frontier life.

Turner might never have emerged as a kind of All-American oracle for all that had it not been for a professor of history named William Francis Allen, who captured Turner's imagination at college and encouraged his flair for research. The University of Wisconsin was a backwater of academia when Turner, a pleasant, optimistic, open-faced little fellow (five feet eight, 130 pounds) reported there as a sub-freshman in the autumn of 1878. But William Allen was an unusual teacher for his day. He spurned both memorization and recital and instead forced his students to dig out source material and to prepare maps and charts to illustrate topics in history they had explored on their own. He made Turner conscious of Darwin—and of the fact that societies evolve as ceaselessly as biological forms—and made room for him as an instructor for two postgraduate years in which the young man, who now aspired to be a historian himself, earned a master's degree.

President Charles W. Eliot of Harvard had recently warned young academics that any who hoped to make

a living teaching history would be engaging in the "height of imprudence." The subject did not attract great academic attention: there were but 15 full professors devoted to it, in fact, in the entire country. But Johns Hopkins University, where Turner went for a doctorate, was different. Herbert Baxter Adams, who taught there, was a man of enthusiasm and ambition. He embraced a view of American history known as the germ theory, which held that American democracy grew from a seed, or germ, that could be traced to Teutonic tribesmen in ancient Germany. And he had attracted brilliant graduate students who labored with him to lay down new "scientific" concepts of history.

Turner gained more than his doctorate in Baltimore; he also built the confidence to rebel against Adams' curious theory. He was vastly encouraged by Woodrow Wilson, who was on leave from the faculty at Wesleyan to teach a course at Johns Hopkins. The two men lived at the same boardinghouse, ate together, took long walks together and shared a common indignation: Wilson, a Southerner, was as certain as his friend from Wisconsin that American history was being throttled by myopic New Englanders and their disregard of events occurring south or west of Boston.

Turner often said, in his later years, that he would never have developed his frontier thesis if he had not been moved to burning rebellion by Herbert Baxter Adams and his fixation on ancient Germany. This seems to have been only partially true. The young historian had come by his interest in the frontier long before meeting Adams. But the "Teutonist" was partly responsible, nevertheless, for Turner's success. Adams was in charge of selecting speakers for a World Congress of Historians, planned as part of the Chicago World's Columbian Exposition of 1893, and he invited Turner, by then on the faculty of the University of Wisconsin, to deliver a paper. Turner was delighted. He had been studying census reports and maps for years and evolving the idea that the westward movement of the frontier amounted to a series of successive rebirths of civilization, a process that had profoundly influenced American society.

No single person present that 12th of July, including the speaker himself, seemed aware that he was party to an event of dazzling significance as Turner rose to deliver the work that was to give so many millions a new consciousness of themselves and their country. The audience, in fact, seemed bored, even comatose— and with reason. It was a hot night; those present in the Chicago Art Institute had already listened to four long discourses (on subjects that included "Early Lead Mining in Illinois and Wisconsin," and "The Social Compact and Mr. Jefferson's Adoption of It").

There was no response—other, apparently, than a stir of relief—as Turner came to his ringing conclusion: "What the Mediterranean Sea was to the Greeks, breaking the bond of custom, offering new experiences, calling out new institutions and activities, that, and more, the ever retreating frontier has been to the United States. . . . And now, four centuries from the discovery of America, at the end of a hundred years of life under the Constitution, the frontier has gone, and with its going has closed the first period of American history."

None in the audience was moved to question the speaker; there was no discussion after he sat down. One Chicago newspaper accorded his presentation a few dutiful lines, but the rest ignored it. A few col-leagues were moved to praise—much of it extremely faint—when the thesis was reprinted by the State Historical Society of Wisconsin in December. Turner had every reason, in the months that followed, to feel that it had been engulfed forever in a sea of silence and indifference. But his frontier thesis developed a life of its own, rose from tiny wavelet to roaring comber in the next decade, and washed across the minds of academicians, publishers and politicians and into the public consciousness with a force that would not be denied.

Few did more to heighten this phenomenon as it materialized than Woodrow Wilson, who accepted, borrowed and recommended his friend's ideas, characterizing him publicly as a man who had earned appreciation, love and support. Gradually other academicians and editors like Walter Hines Page of the *Atlantic Monthly* were struck by the hypothesis and asked its author to speak or write (a process Turner accelerated by mailing copies of his paper to targets of intellectual opportunity). And Turner's students (from Harvard—which hired him away in 1910—as well as from Wisconsin) scattered, over the years, and preached his concepts as Holy Writ.

The thesis sounds obvious today because we have grown so conscious of history, have been so reminded of the Old West, and have been so imbued, as children, with residue of the Turnerian view. But it was seen as revelation in the early 1900s. Historian after historian, professor after professor, high school teacher after high school teacher embraced and exaggerated the new gospel. Millions and millions of new or altered textbooks reflected it; the major student histories between 1830 and 1870 had devoted but 2.2 per cent of their subject matter to the West, but 93 per cent of those published between 1900 and 1925 proclaimed the frontier as the principal force in the nation's development. Sociologists, politicians, economists and businessmen enthusiastically seized upon Turnerism.

Criticism of Turner's thesis was drowned, for decades, in a rumble of approval. The thesis was optimistic (he had predicted that "the expansive character of American life" would not cease with the closing of the frontier, and that "American energy will continually demand a wider field for its exercise"). It was flattering (it allowed Americans to assume that the wilderness had made them a superior people). And it permitted

Buyers flock to San Diego's Ocean Beach in 1887 for an auction of 2,500 lots. As the frontier era came to an end, Westerners whose predecessors had found plenty of open country for homesteading increasingly had to purchase land from speculators who subdivided large tracts.

those worried about the rise of Populism, the imperialistic aftermath of the Spanish-American War, the spread of slums and the inequalities of industrialism to find comforting, if unsubstantiated, faith in the future. American individualism would survive every trial.

Turner had not set out to brew a panacea for the nation's ills but simply to advance a reasonable hypothesis for testing by historians. He did not suggest that American society had been shaped solely by the frontier. But the professor's excited disciples converted his concept into inviolable social gospel. Reaction was inevitable as the Great Depression fell upon a country already disillusioned by World War I, and made dogma based on the character and accomplishments of trappers and backwoodsmen seem remote and unreal.

Scholars hacked away at the famous thesis like Sioux on the warpath. Turner was accused of ignoring obvious European contributions to American culture, of forgetting the influence of industrialization in molding American society, and of having naïvely swallowed unproven theories of environmental determinism. New Dealers derided Turnerism's faith in individuality and self-reliance as a fallacious credo during years in which F.D.R.'s alphabet bureaus were conceived as safety valves for an economy that industrialists could not maintain, and in which dust storms beset the prairies once heralded as a source of national salvation.

But Turner's message endured. Scholars recognized him again, once the outcries of the 1930s and 1940s had subsided, as a man who revolutionized the study of the American past. The essentials of his thesis are known to millions who would not recognize his name. His views penetrated so deeply into the national consciousness in the early 1900s, and became so entangled with Western mythology as it was recited by bards more raffish by far than he, that his concept of the frontier seems irretrievably locked into the amalgam of fact and fancy that has become the American epic. In a sense, thus, he is one with movie cowboys, Western entrepreneurs who trade in nostalgia, rodeo ropers and those writers, past and present, who have reconstructed the Old West to fit their own dreams.

Sagas draw up improbability as plants draw up water, but from the beginning the vast, heroic folk tale of the American West was force-fed improbability by means

The quake that rocked San Francisco out of the Old West

No part of the old, boomtown West of the 1800s was more rudely jolted into the 20th Century than was San Francisco on the morning of April 18, 1906. At 5:12 a.m., "the city shook like an aspen leaf," reported the *Los Angeles Times,* "and her grey highways suddenly cracked and split as though batteries of Satan and his upper hell had been opened."

A sudden 20-foot shift of the earth along the San Andreas Fault had set off an earthquake that had the power of more than 12 million tons of exploding TNT. In just over one minute, much of the city of San Francisco was reduced to a heap of splintered houses, fallen chimneys and lifeless bodies.

But the quake itself was only the beginning. San Francisco's many wooden structures made the city a tinderbox; houses, saloons and stores rapidly burst into flames as soot loosened by the quake fell down chimneys, scattering fire into rooms. By 9 a.m., more than 50 separate major fires were sweeping through the ravaged city. After sunset the flames made the sky so luminous that observers who were 50 miles away claimed that they "could read a newspaper at midnight."

After the smoke cleared three days later, 450 persons were found to be dead and 200,000 homeless, and 28,000 buildings lay in ruins. With typical Western resilience, San Franciscans rallied and started to rebuild. However, an irreplaceable part of the Old West—the sections of San Francisco that were redolent of the gaudy, bawdy gold-rush era— was gone forever. In its place rose a modern city. By 1909, more than half of all the steel and concrete buildings that existed at that point in America stood in San Francisco, tall against the Western sky of a new age.

San Franciscans survey the smouldering ruins of their city from Telegraph Hill four days

after the 1906 earthquake. Ruptured mains, spewing forth millions of gallons of water, left firemen helpless to defend the burning city.

denied the legends of earlier civilizations. Settlement of the West coincided, roughly, with the adoption of the steam-powered, high-speed rotary press, and with an expansion of public education for the poor and middle-class children of big cities (appropriations for New York City's common schools tripled between 1860 and 1869) who demanded racier prose than the Sunday School literature being produced for offspring of the wealthy. At about the same time the Civil War created a thirst for cheap, sensational reading matter in millions of soldiers seeking surcease from boredom between battles. Brigades of ink-stained wretches—many of whom had never traveled beyond Hoboken, New Jersey—turned to whacking out dime novels as a result, and created a highly imaginary Wild West that survives in television reruns to this day.

Dozens of entrepreneurs set out to get rich quick by way of this "steam literature"—so called after the steam presses that printed it. M. M. Ballou of Boston, Carey & Hart of Philadelphia, Frederick A. Brady of New York were only a few of the publishers who fought for nickels and dimes with titles like *Tricks and Traps of New York, The Stranger's Grave* and, to name an early Western, *Jack Long, or Shot in the Eye, a True Story of Texas Border Life*. But many of these impresarios vanished overnight—dime publishing was a cutthroat business—and all of them were overshadowed in the end by Erastus Flavel Beadle, a country boy who made himself a captain of industry.

Beadle discovered that there was money in words while apprenticed to a miller in western New York state: he got a penny apiece for carving hardwood typefaces that were used in stamping flour bags. He then went off to Cooperstown to learn the printer's trade, moved to Buffalo to practice it and—after succeeding with a little magazine called *Beadle's Home Monthly*—invaded New York City to seek his fortune. He was lucky. With his brother Irwin P. Beadle he produced an early cheap novel, *Malaeska, the Indian Wife of the White Hunter,* which sold in the hundreds of thousands. Erastus Beadle had an instinct for the marketplace that many of his competitors lacked. He paid authors on the dot in a day when many publishers stole manuscripts that arrived in the mail. He used placards and street sandwich men to advertise, and he bound his books with bright, salmon-colored

covers, which allowed the buyer to recognize them immediately at a range of 50 yards.

Beadle dominated dime publishing until 1889—the year he retired to a grand estate, Glimmerview, at Cooperstown. He defended steam literature against charges of immorality from the pulpit—dime novels being considered by some as sinister a threat to American youth as nicotine—with a piety that matched that of his critics. But his editorial attitudes did not differ widely from those of his competitors for all that. All sought to capture the same public—largely composed of Easterners—and all fed it Western melodrama, which was at ludicrous odds with reality.

Most of the scribblers who turned out these little books had specialized in thrillers about spies, pirates, soldiers and dashing young elitists before and during the Civil War and most of them simply transferred such characters to Texas or the Dakotas, borrowing heavily from the *Leatherstocking Tales,* when first directed to produce stories of Western adventure. The results were odd indeed. Their heroes and heroines spoke an outrageous sort of frontier lingo, but usually proved—since they had been going about in disguise—to be highly moral and of good family. They persisted in wearing coonskin caps and in carrying flintlock rifles for years after real Westerners were banging away with Colts and Winchesters; when this phase had passed they were sometimes accoutered in velvet jackets, bright sashes, golden spurs and other gaudy costumes.

The cowboy seldom played a leading role in early dime novels, which were populated by hunters and scouts like Duke Darrall and Texas lawmen like Moccasin Mat. Duke was a handsome devil who wore buckskin suits and had a fantastic sense of balance—he was able to hop about, standing erect, upon the backs of stampeding mustangs and to guide them easily from this point of vantage. It was suggested that he was a gentleman of natural nobility despite his rough exterior, since he sent beautiful Wilna, a white girl who had been captured by Indians, off to a St. Louis seminary for two years before marrying her. Moccasin Mat was equally high-toned and romantic. He was not only permitted to speak good English (or English as good, at any rate, as author Harry St. George could provide) but to possess a horse, Storm Cloud, which ran up like a dog when he whistled, and a long-lost sweetheart,

A Nebraska sodbuster chats on his new telephone around the turn of the century. Telephone service did much to ameliorate the loneliness of families living on farms in the West and brought help in emergencies that formerly had to be faced alone.

Hattie Farley, who behaved in much the same fashion after being reunited with him.

The dime houses titillated their public further, as time went on, with desperate, if uniformly beautiful, heroines, who spent a good deal of time galloping around disguised as men. There was Pepita, for instance—also known as Nebraska Larry—who invaded the gambling hells of Omaha, "the hardest place east of Denver," seeking vengeance on a rotter who had wronged her in the past.

Many of these wild women proved to be both feminine and socially acceptable when the reader was permitted closer looks at their innate characters. Calamity Jane in *The Heroine of Whoop-Up* could "drink whiskey, shute, play keerds, or sw'ar, ef et comes ter et" but revealed "a breast of alabaster purity" on occasions when her rough shirt was allowed to fall open. Dove-Eye, alias Kate Robinette, a half-Indian maiden, rode astride and threw a battle-ax at Fred Wilder, the hero, before (1) inheriting a large fortune and (2) falling in love with Fred (whom she had fortunately missed in their initial encounter). But when Fred's father suggested that she be sent to St. Louis for the seminary treatment like beautiful Wilna, Fred insisted, manfully, that "she is sufficiently polished, and no one can educate her better than her husband."

But the West of the dime novel cannot be fully savored through such encapsulation of plot; its characters engaged in a kind of dialogue—exemplified by the following lines lifted from *Old Bull's Eye, the Lightning Shot of the Plains*—that made them unique, to put it mildly, in American literature:

" 'At last, Antone Barillo—at last!'

"The words sounded like a death-knell. With a low, inarticulate cry, the wretched ranchero strove to arise, but then he fell back, his face livid, a bloody froth gathering upon his lips. It seemed as though the hand of death was upon him.

"Old Bull's Eye dropped the torch and bent forward, his face white with a terrible hatred.

" 'Antone Barillo—thief, murderer! where are my wife and child? Speak, or by the God above! I will tear your false heart out with my naked hands! Speak!' "

The authors of these potboilers cranked out hundreds of fictitious works about real, in addition to imaginary, Westerners: Kit Carson, Wild Bill Hickok, Joaquin Marieta, George Armstrong Custer and, of course, Buffalo Bill Cody (of whom more later) and involved them in feats of derring-do that would have tried the constitution of Superman himself. Most of these heroes of the plains accepted their fictional counterparts with good grace, even gratitude, although Carson was moved to observe that one of his biographers had "laid it on a leetle too thick." Readers, as a result, sometimes tended to believe that some purely imaginary heroes were real as well—particularly Deadwood Dick, the invention of one Edward L. Wheeler, a mild-mannered man who called his acquaintants "pard" but never got west of Illinois.

Deadwood was a kind of latter-day Robin Hood who dressed like an early Lone Ranger. He wore buckskin of "jetty black" and a "thick black veil through the eyeholes of which there gleamed a pair of orbs of piercing intensity." But he turned up so often, since Beadle and Adams produced 33 books about him—and another 97 about his son Deadwood Dick Jr., a character virtually indistinguishable from his fictional father—that some admirers were convinced that he was actually coursing the prairies out yonder as they followed his adventures in print.

Deadwood was the first dime-novel hero who was an outlaw, albeit one with a means of rationalizing his banditry. He had been wronged by powerful villains who, because they were members of the establishment, were supported by the law. He sought revenge and justice, which made him popular with working-class readers who felt oppressed by 19th Century industrialism and the bosses who ruled their lives. Deadwood Dick's huge and instantaneous success inspired other publishing houses to make heroes out of bandits—even real ones, including the infamous Frank and Jesse James. Protests by pious citizens and actions by the postmaster general—who threatened to withdraw publishers' second-class mailing privileges—eventually contained the exploitation of this popularly successful trend in dime novels, but by then the heroic outlaw had taken root in Western myth, destined to flower in later fiction, movies and television.

Deadwood Dick and Erastus Beadle lasted just about as long as the actual frontier (Deadwood Dick's author died in 1885, the retired publisher in 1894). Their successors based fancy on fact in contriving the

Western legend—of circling wagon trains, of the U.S. Cavalry, of beautiful, pure ranchers' daughters, of villainous rustlers and hard-bitten cowboys—that succeeded that of Dove-Eye and Moccasin Mat.

The publishing house of Street & Smith—which had devoted itself to paperbacks about Buffalo Bill in the declining years of the dime novel—funneled these epic themes into a new mass medium by launching the pulp paper *Western Story Magazine* in 1919. Dozens of other Western pulps evolved (*Ace-High Magazine, Super Western, Cowboy Stories, Crack Shot Western, Texas Rangers* and *Wild West Weekly* among them) and a school of high-speed writers (including Frederick Faust—alias Max Brand—Clarence E. Mulford, Frank Richardson Pierce and W. C. Tuttle) sprang up to feed them. The vogue for their "rip roaring" stories and serials lasted 30 years.

The pulps strove for a realism of background and method that the dime novels had never attempted. Their cowboys breathed the dust of real roundups, their pioneers crossed rivers easily located on maps, and their rustlers altered brands and evaded capture as convincingly as any ever pursued by the Wyoming Cattlemen's Association. The pulp reader was able to learn that the Colt Peacemaker was Model 1873, that the Winchester carbine of 1894 came in three calibers (.32-40, .38-40 and .44-40) and was treated to an endless lexicon of Western terms: riding drag (the dusty position behind a herd of cattle on the trail), latigo (the strap that attaches the saddle to the cinch), night-wrangler (the man guarding a trail crew's horses at night), ramada (a brush shelter), ring herding (moving cattle continually in a circle to prevent their scattering). But the rip-roaring school of writers overdramatized and romanticized the West nonetheless.

More serious writers were also carried into romanticism—almost, it seemed despite themselves—when dealing with the West. This was true of Owen Wister and his towering bestseller, *The Virginian*. Wister's hero seems destined to live forever, if only by virtue of one line: "When you call me that, *smile!*" uttered after the villain, Trampas, called him, as Wister spelled it for a sensitive readership, a son-of-a---- over cards in a Medicine Bow saloon.

The Virginian had a certain monosyllabic quality and a style—"His broad, soft hat was pushed back . . . and one casual thumb was hooked in the cartridge belt that slanted across his hips. . . ."—that came to be accepted as authentically Western, and were later reflected by a young actor from Montana named Gary Cooper. But Wister saw Westerners through a hero worshipper's eyes—so much so that he refused to wear chaps while living in the West because he did not feel entitled to such a badge of frontier life—and his cowboy is a kind of parfit gentle knight of the range who is never seen in actual contact with cows.

Most other Americans—from the historian Turner to the Okies of the Great Depression—who have headed west in imagination or in fact and have become involved in the saga that has shaped us all, have fallen willingly to the same spell. It is hard not to conclude that the supreme artificer of this American epic was that Ohio dentist-turned-author, Zane Grey, who made no discernible attempt to restrain the romantic emotionalism of his response to Western landscapes, Western history and Western men.

Grey was an avaricious reader of Beadle novels as a boy in Zanesville, Ohio, a star baseball player at the University of Pennsylvania, and a reluctant scholar who seems to have studied—and later practiced—dentistry with no more than an aimless if nagging sense of duty. But he was galvanized by the vast, sere vistas of the West on a trip to Arizona in the early 1900s and used them, for the rest of his life, as backdrops for novels in which heroic men fought nature and the schemes of equally stereotyped villains. Grey's work falls short of most standards of literary criticism, but must be judged seriously as a reflection of myth and legend—which encompass a people's most uncritical dreams of itself—for its very faults.

"Mr. Grey's work is a primitive epic and has the characteristics of other primitive epics," wrote T. K. Whipple, one of the few critics who neither ignored nor ridiculed the author. "If he must be classified let it be with the authors of *Beowulf* or the Icelandic sagas." Grey's novels (among them *To the Last Man, Wanderer of the Wasteland, West of the Pecos*) outsold all other books except the Bible and McGuffey's readers during his lifetime. The heroine of his *Riders of the Purple Sage* spoke for America in 1912 when she stared into the desert and hoped that "out of those lovely purple reaches . . . might ride a fearless man. . . ."

An uneasy role for a proud people

"This civilization may not be the best possible," mused the Commissioner of Indian Affairs in 1889 about the white world that had engulfed his charges, "but it is the best the Indians can get. They cannot escape it, and must either conform to it or be crushed by it." This brutally frank statement of the Indian's fate omitted one crucial observation: that conforming and being crushed could be the same thing.

Already demoralized by their confinement on reservations, Indians found themselves beset by whites determined to exact conformity. Zealous missionaries pursued Indian souls while trying to put a stop to tribal religious practices. Indian children were sent to schools where they were punished for speaking their native tongues.

Without buffalo, Plains Indians had to subsist on government rations. For a while beef rations arrived on the hoof, and Indians tried to revive some semblance of their traditional bison hunts by slaying the cattle from horseback. But after complaints from whites who witnessed the slaughter, this "barbarism" was officially forbidden.

By the end of the century the Indian had become but a poor imitator of his ancestors, posing as the warrior he no longer was and performing once-sacred rituals for the benefit of gawking pale-face tourists. He was at ease with neither the white culture nor his own heritage. Much later in the 20th Century Indian pride would come to life again. But for decades it languished, victim of a scheme that was meant, in the words of one white do-gooder, to "kill the Indian and save the man."

Former Sioux warriors, in full regalia, express guarded amusement aboard the first automobile to appear on South Dakota's Rosebud reservation around 1910.

A mounted Indian uses sign language to direct participants in a Fourth of July celebration on a Montana reservation about 1905. For many tribes, Independence Day festivities substituted in part for banned traditional ceremonies.

38

Indian women display crafts for sale to browsing shoppers in Juneau, Alaska, at the turn of the century. Although the white man's profit system was adopted as a means of survival, it was repugnant to most Indians, who believed that possessions were accumulated merely to be given away.

41

Self-conscious Hopi snake dancers perform for fashionably dressed tourists in 1902. The intrusive white man's camera was eventually banned from such rites—a last-ditch attempt by the Indians to preserve a measure of dignity.

43

2 | Show time for the West

In 1883, the West came east when frontier scout and dime-novel hero Buffalo Bill Cody took to the road with his first Wild West show. Heralded by a bright splash of gaudy show bills—the beginning of a flood of Wild West show publicity that would soon engulf the country—Buffalo Bill presented his audiences with three action-packed hours of marksmanship, horsemanship and frontier derring-do that symbolized the West to everyone who saw the extravaganzas.

Cody's success at wrapping up the West into a marketable package inspired more than a hundred imitators. From shoestring operations to huge shows with their own trains, these companies studiously copied Cody's buckskin-clad scouts, sharpshooting cowboys and war-bonneted Indians and promoted performances with the flashiest posters they could afford.

The major shows commissioned attractive lithographs of their star acts; smaller shows bought stock paper printed with Wild West scenes and added their names. For weeks before a show came to town, advance men—up to three railway cars full for Buffalo Bill—would blanket the area with posters ranging from small handbills to enormous, multisheet emblazonments that could cover the side of a barn or up to 140 feet of running fence. Almost as much as the shows they advertised, these posters reinforced the myth of a gloriously romantic and glamorous American frontier that had not existed until it appeared in the dusty arena of Buffalo Bill's Wild West.

Braced against his fallen horse, a surrounded but undaunted Buffalo Bill fires coolly into a band of Indians. This poster, which was probably used to promote the 1894 season, dramatizes the dime-novel heroics of Cody, rather than an act in the show.

BUFFALO B
AND CONGRESS OF ROUG

COL. W. F. COD

LL'S WILD WEST
RIDERS OF THE WORLD.

A. Hoen & Co Baltimore U.S.A.

(BUFFALO BILL) A CLOSE CALL.

TIGER BILLS

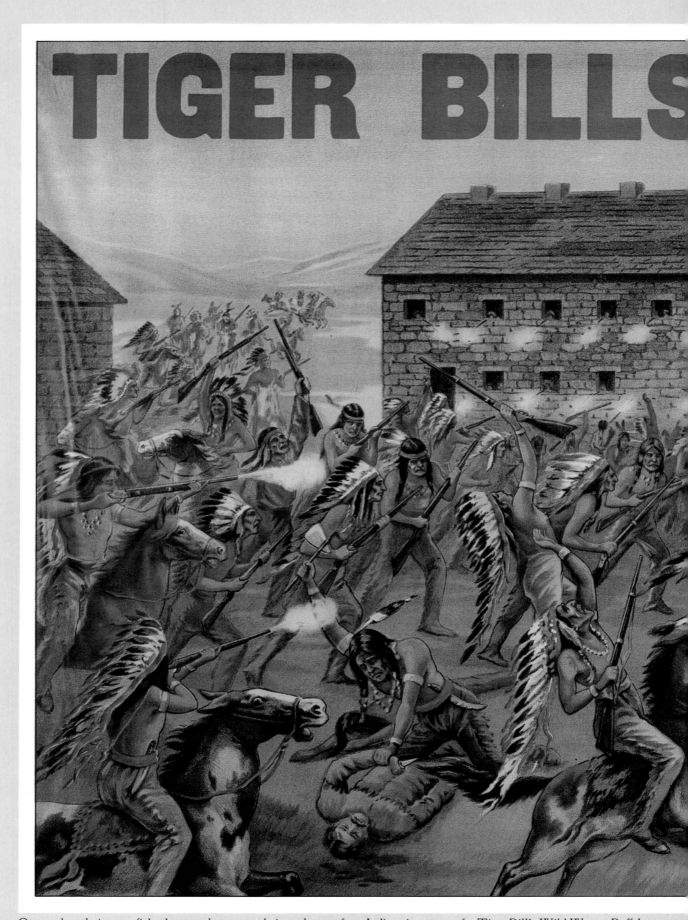

Outnumbered pioneers fight desperately to save their settlement from Indians in a poster for Tiger Bill's Wild West, a Buffalo

WILD WEST

Bill-style show that toured the U.S. from 1909 through 1934. Indian attacks were standard acts in most Wild West shows.

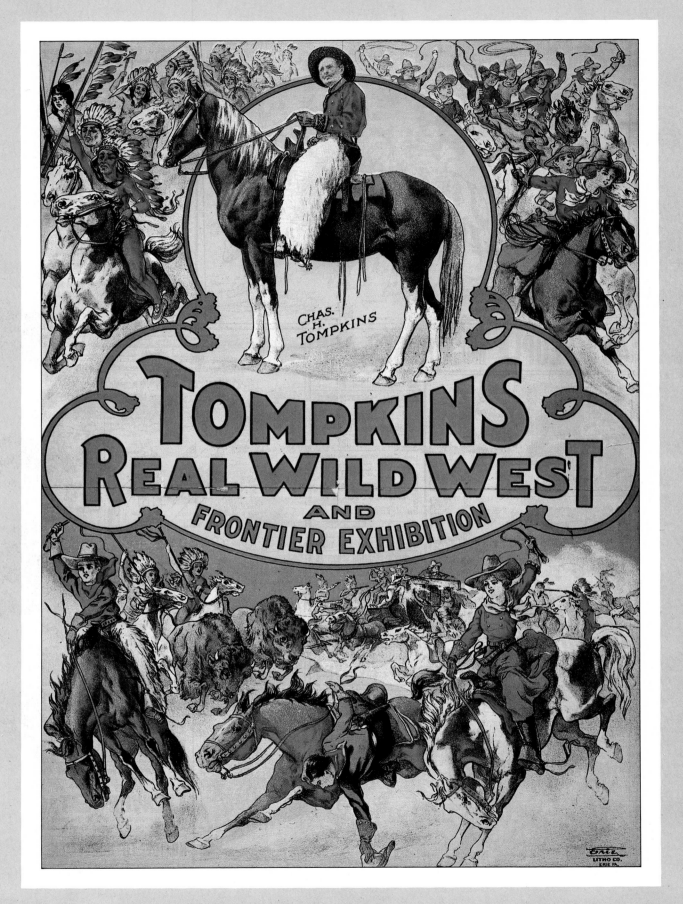

Charles H. Tompkins, surrounded in this poster by whooping members of his frontier troupe, was a Texas cowboy until he was discovered by a Wild West talent scout in the late 1880s. He became a star roper and rider with Buffalo Bill and in 1910 formed his own Wild West show.

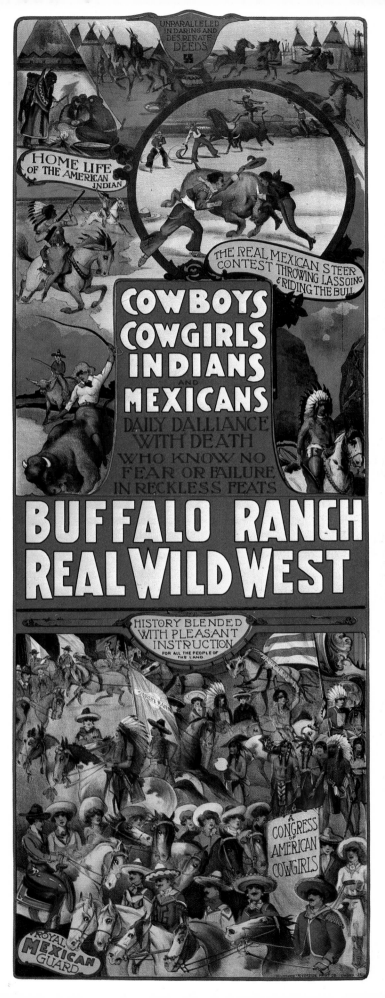

A poster for Buffalo Ranch, a name used by several different shows between 1910 and 1934, advertises the theatrical antics of its cowboys, cowgirls, Indians and Mexicans as both historical and instructive. Most of the audiences believed that the standard Wild West exaggerations were accurate slices of frontier life.

A genuine Indian village was featured in movie cowboy Tim McCoy's exhibition. Formed in 1938, it was the last

major Wild West show. Audiences preferred thrills, not anthropology, and the show was bankrupt within a month.

The old scout who gave romance to the Western myth

A gnomelike little fellow named Edward Z. C. Judson ("Colonel" Judson, he liked to say when impressing the unwary) got off a Union Pacific train at North Platte, Nebraska, in late July, 1869, took a carriage to the town's satellite Army post, Fort McPherson, and prepared to confer an enormous privilege upon one Frank North, a major commanding the district's Pawnee Scouts. Judson introduced himself as a fellow warrior but confessed he was also Ned Buntline, king of the dime novelists. He had heard North credited with killing a chief named Tall Bull in an attack on Sioux and Cheyenne renegades at Summit Springs, Colorado, and had hastened to his side to make him a hero of popular literature. North simply grunted. "If you want a man to fill *that* bill," he said, finally, "He's over there under that wagon."

Judson—no whit discouraged, to use his own prose style—walked, limping from an old injury, to the heavy Army vehicle the officer had indicated and peered beneath it. It was a hot day; a big, flushed, handsome young roughneck was asleep in the wagon's shade with flies crawling on his face. Judson prodded him awake and introduced himself. William Frederick Cody, a scout for General Eugene A. Carr of the Fifth U.S. Cavalry, crawled out, knocking hay from his thick brown hair, and shook hands with Opportunity.

Such was the momentous first encounter between Ned Buntline and Buffalo Bill—at least according to tradition. Old records suggest that the men initially met each other in entirely different fashion: that Judson stopped at the fort simply to pass the time before de-

livering a temperance lecture at nearby Cottonwood Springs, that he did not hunt up Major North (who may well have been visiting his home at Columbus, Nebraska, at the time) and that he encountered Cody only because a Major William H. Brown, who was chatting with the writer, called the scout over and said, casually, "Cody, allow me to introduce Colonel Judson, otherwise known as Ned Buntline." But whether or not Cody actually crawled from beneath a wagon, there is no doubt that he emerged into the limelight of world acclaim at Judson's nudging.

Cody was 23 when the pair met; Judson was 46. Cody was a fellow with an instinct for the main chance, "vain as a woman at Easter" (in the words of a later biographer) and devoted to marathon drunks. But he was also a dead shot, a brave man and further, in the opinion of General Carr, a great tracker "with eyesight better than a field glass." Judson was one of the greatest liars ever born, but for all his bombast he was as combative as a wildcat. They took to each other. The plainsman invited Judson along on a "scout," told him about the action at Summit Springs—where Cody, not North, had killed Chief Tall Bull, according to most witnesses—and allowed the novelist to ride his horse, Powder Face. Judson showed off his scars, told untruths about storming the walls of Montezuma (he had never even been in Mexico) and went back east, where he wrote the first of 557 dime novels (exclusive of several hundred more in foreign languages) that he and others would turn out about a hero of the plains by the name of Buffalo Bill.

Judson did not invent the name. There had been a dozen Buffalo Bills drifting about the prairies after the Civil War. But there was only one by the time Buntline was through launching Cody on a career that would make him one of the most celebrated Americans of his day, earn him fortunes, and make the American

---

Buffalo Bill Cody, scout turned showman, relaxes in his tent. At first doubtful about entering show business, he once told a theater manager, "You might as well try to make an actor out of a government mule."

53

frontier an entertainment spectacle for fascinated millions around the world.

Fate could not have chosen a more colorful agent to orchestrate Cody's transformation from a rough young plainsman into a key figure of Western mythology. Judson was a genuine desperado as well as an inventive egomaniac and had survived real escapades as lurid as those he attributed to his new friend. Relatives attending the christening of Edward Zane Carroll Judson in 1823 would have had every reason for expecting the infant to lead a life of circumspection and rectitude. His family was composed of upright, middle-class upstate New Yorkers. His father, Levi Judson, was a stern schoolmaster-turned-lawyer who published works on morals and patriotism.

But Edward ran away to sea as a lad of 13, wangled his way into the Navy and was commissioned a midshipman two years later for saving the crew of a ship's boat that overturned in New York's East River. He was moved to incessant pranks—often to spite other young officers who resented his promotion from the lower deck—and got stories about some of them published in *Knickerbocker Magazine,* under the pseudonym Ned Buntline. He left the Navy a few years later and started a sensational paper, *Ned Buntline's Own,* at Nashville, Tennessee, but abandoned the project under duress after having shot to death one Robert Porterfield when the man accused him of wife-stealing.

Porterfield's brother shot Judson in the chest in return, and a lynch mob bent on avenging Porterfield's death pursued the wounded writer into the City Hotel. Judson leaped ("47 feet, 3 inches," he claimed) from a high window, damaging one leg for life, was jailed, taken out of his cell, hanged from an awning post, cut down by an anonymous Samaritan, taken back to jail and eventually—after a grand jury failed to indict—was allowed to slip out of town. He was shortly in New York, leading an anti-immigrant mob that precipitated a riot in which 34 men were killed and 141 wounded. He served a year and a day on Blackwell's Island for his pains, was given a parade by his friends on release, became a leader of the Know-Nothing Party and escaped trial for starting another riot in St. Louis by jumping bail.

He wrote continuously while embroiled in such adventures, made $20,000 a year, acquired and shucked

off a series of wives and mistresses, kept a steam yacht in the East River and elevated himself to the rank of colonel after desultory service in the Civil War (much of it as a deserter and a member of the Invalid Reserves). He also claimed that he had been the Union Army's Chief of Indian Scouts.

Judson did not hesitate, having thus reinvented himself, to create a new character for his friend Cody in the first of the novels, *Buffalo Bill, the King of the Bordermen.* In the book the plainsman's old mother (who, in fact, was dead) and Wild Bill Hickok (whom the author had never met) gave testimony to Cody's sterling qualities:

"Better son never blessed a mother, wild as he was. Rough he may be to others, but to us he is kind and gentle as the breeze of a summer eve."

"Yes, ma-am," answered Wild Bill, "as good as ever made, no matter whar you find him. There isn't a bit of white in his liver, nor black in his heart."

Buffalo Bill was also portrayed (to Cody's profane amazement upon reading the finished work) as a mighty warrior crusading in the cause of temperance. "There is more fight, more headache—aye, more *heart* ache in one rum bottle than there is in all the water that

In this thriller, author Buntline had Bill, "the People's Hero," tell an Indian maiden why he must pursue a gang of woman-snatchers: "It is my duty to your sex, my manhood, and to the Great Spirit."

The rascally writer Ned Buntline was an accomplished marksman. However, the heroics he ascribed to Bill Cody were so far off target that the hero, though appreciative, did not recognize himself at first.

Dr. William F. Carver, Cody's first partner and costar, was quick-tempered and very jealous of rivals. Once, after missing a target in a show, he smashed his rifle over his horse's ears and punched his assistant.

ever sparkled in God's bright sunlight. And I, for the sake of my dear brothers and sisters, and for the sweet, trusting heart that throbs for me alone" — a reference to Bill's wife, Louisa Frederici Cody, who certainly knew better — "intend to let the rum go where it belongs and that is not down my throat."

Of course Buffalo Bill did not drink! He needed a steady hand and a keen eye for his valorous and dangerous exploits. Not that the fictionalized Bill was a man to brag about his deeds. He modestly attributed much of his success to his horse, Powder Face, "for that pony can out-smell, out-see, and out-hear any living thing, be it man, dog or catamount. Look at him standing there, one eye open and t'other one shut — but see how his ears pint. He knows I'm talking about him. Isn't he a rare insect? He can run ten hours and never flag, swim any current this side of the big hills and knows as much as I do about hide and seek. Powder Face, go bring

your saddle and bridle — we're going on a scout."

This ornate and splendidly inaccurate first novel devoted to Buffalo Bill was converted into a play and enacted at Niblo's Gardens on the Bowery after being serialized in the *New York Weekly* as "the wildest, truest story Ned Buntline ever wrote." Judson soon whacked out a trio of sequels: *Buffalo Bill's Best Shot, or the Heart of Spotted Tail; Buffalo Bill's Last Victory, or Dove Eye the Lodge Queen;* and *Hazel Eye, the Girl Trapper.*

Few Westerners of the day had been privy to a more thorough grounding in the real rigors of the frontier than the man Buntline chose to immortalize. Cody was born on a farm in Scott County, Iowa Territory, on February 26, 1846, but was taken to the plains of Kansas at age eight. He was thrown on his own resources there at 11 when his father, Isaac, an outspoken abolitionist, died of complications after being stabbed by an equally fevered advocate of slavery on Kansas soil. Bill found work as a drover for westbound wagon trains, rubbed shoulders with Jim Bridger and Kit Carson at Fort Laramie, became a Pony Express rider, hunted Indians on the Powder River with James Butler (later Wild Bill) Hickok, and spent the last year of the Civil War as an enlisted soldier of the Seventh Kansas Volunteers, having joined up at 18 while too drunk to realize what he was doing.

He was back on the plains, exercising his skills as hunter, tracker and Indian-fighter almost as soon as the war ended. His haste to return to his work was in no small part inspired by a desire to escape the domesticity in which he found himself trapped after winning and marrying Louisa Frederici, a hot-tempered young woman he met during an Army furlough in St. Louis. Cody was entranced when Louisa's cousin, a fellow soldier, introduced him to her in the Frederici parlor: he had never before encountered a "cultivated" young lady. Louisa was equally enthralled: she not only thought Cody the handsomest man she had ever seen, but deluded herself into believing she could convert him into the sort of frugal, hard-working, conservative husband her Alsatian family expected her to marry. She was soon disabused, though her new husband tried — at least temporarily — to meet her expectations.

The newly wed Cody opened a boardinghouse he called the Golden Rule Hotel at Salt Creek, Kansas.

He went broke in a hurry, however, through his excessively literal interpretation of the establishment's name—buying drinks on the house for his thirsty friends and freeloading relatives. Louisa wept and raged. Cody fled, got drunk with his old friend, Wild Bill, and turned to shooting buffalo for the tables of Kansas Pacific Railroad construction camps—in which work he acquired his nickname—and to shepherding cavalry detachments on raids in Indian country.

He had proved himself a remarkable Indian-fighter and scout in nine battles with the Fifth Cavalry and had been chosen by General Phil Sheridan himself as a guide for influential toffs—among them the Earl of Dunraven, the *New York Herald*'s Editor James Gordon Bennett Jr. and Russia's Grand Duke Alexis—who wanted the Army to help them shoot buffalo before the big beasts all disappeared for good. Sheridan, who lauded Cody for "courage and endurance," could have chosen no guide more competent for tenderfeet intent on finding big game. And Buffalo Bill, although he was only semiliterate and had very little knowledge of the social niceties, revealed subtleties of manner when he started to mingle with the rich and famous: poise, a kind of rough, intuitive urbanity and a surprising ability to attract, impress and entertain the worldly and the powerful.

Cody began to acquire the techniques of a showman while responding to the atmosphere of opulence engendered by these curious expeditions. The Army overlooked no luxury in providing for famous guests—16 wagons full of tents and supplies, including two to carry ice and wine, awaited Bennett's party, and Sheridan furnished 100 troopers of the Fifth Cavalry as bodyguards and outriders. Cody arrayed himself in a crimson shirt and a white buckskin suit, clapped a white sombrero on his shoulder-length ringlets and mounted a "gallant white stepper" before galloping up to be introduced to his new charges. The toffs were captivated. Grand Duke Alexis presented his guide with a fur coat and a set of jeweled studs and cuff links on parting, and Bennett insisted on paying for Cody to travel to New York City, housing him at the Union Club and exhibiting him in white tie and tails at balls, operas and banquets for six giddy weeks.

The new social lion went back west to join the Third Cavalry—arriving at Fort McPherson in a fash-

ionable claw-hammer coat and a stovepipe hat, still jovially soused from a party at Omaha. He missed the heady ring of acclaim, however, and went east once again with Texas Jack Omohundro, a fellow scout, when Judson invited the pair to go to Chicago in order to play themselves in a melodrama entitled *Scouts of the Prairie*.

Judson had neglected to write the play before Cody's arrival, but he managed to concoct it within four hours (with a part for himself that allowed delivery of a temperance lecture), hired an Italian dancer to take the role of Dove Eye, a Beautiful Indian Maiden, and contrived her fellow tribesmen (whom he billed in advance as genuine Pawnee chiefs) by dressing a dozen Chicago bums in brown cambric pantalets and daubing them liberally with war paint. The resultant production, which opened at Nixon's Ampitheater on December 18, 1872, was probably one of the most atro-

Buffalo Bill, after galloping into an Omaha arena at the head of an imposing force of horsemen, doffs his hat to the audience. By 1907, when this picture was made, his brown hair had turned snowy white.

cious theatrical endeavors that ever appeared on the American stage.

"Incongruous drama . . . execrable acting," wrote one critic. "So wonderful in its feebleness," concluded another, "that no ordinary intellect can comprehend it." But it was noisy: the Indians were lassoed, en masse, amid blood-curdling screams in act 2 and were killed off with blank cartridges in act 3. And it made money, grossing $16,200 during one week in Boston alone, when it went on the road.

Cody himself was a tremendous hit—although he was paralyzed by stage fright at first and betrayed "the diffidence of a school boy" when he finally opened his mouth. Crowds jammed theaters simply to look at him, and the audience applauded like mad when he cried, sheepishly (at a performance attended by his wife in St.

Louis), "Oh, Mama . . . I'm a *bad* actor!" New York reporters admired his looks, praised his "lithe, springy step" and "realism" and even seemed refreshed by his "uncultured voice and utter absence of stage art," though they thought the play itself was a "very poor slop," and one of them wrote cuttingly of Buntline's "maundering imbecility."

Cody, too, thought the play was nonsense, was embarrassed by his own clumsy attempts at acting, and broke with Judson in the spring after making only $6,000 for his season's labors. Nevertheless, he lusted for the sound of applause, and he was shrewd enough to suspect that the clamoring public might make him rich if properly encouraged. He resolved to take to the road again with a new play, *Scouts of the Plains,* when a press agent named John M. (Arizona John) Burke

agreed to manage the company. Burke thought Cody was the greatest man ever born ("I have met a god in the zenith of his manhood . . . the finest specimen of God's handiwork I have ever seen") and was to stick with him for more than three decades. Burke was a genius at scrounging publicity and he enticed crowds to the show with continuous notices in newspapers. Cody spent the greater part of the next eight years traveling from one dreary dressing room to the next—unable to resist the ring of acclaim and the lure of "money to throw to the birds."

Not that his life lacked excitement. He talked Wild Bill Hickok into joining the troupe, for one thing—an innovation that proved to be unwise from the moment that Hickok arrived at the Brevoort Hotel in New York City and flattened a hack driver for asking what

Wild Bill considered an irrational fare. Hickok complained that he was being asked to play the fool, threw his pistol at a spotlight and shattered it when he was first exposed to its glare, demanded real whiskey out loud when he was presented with cold tea during a drinking scene on stage, and battered a gang of half a dozen oil-field roughnecks with a chair in a barroom during a stopover at Titusville, Pennsylvania. Wild Bill deserted—to the relief of all concerned—at Rochester, New York, after pulling a stagehand aside and muttering, "Tell that long haired son of a bitch I have no more use for him or his damned show business."

Cody abandoned the stage himself—unable to tolerate such "mockery" after his six-year-old son, Kit Carson Cody, died of scarlet fever in the spring of 1876—and headed west once again to help the Army

Amid the noise of gun blasts, screams and war whoops, scores of soldiers and Indians present this scene of frightening carnage in the

Wild West arena. Cody's audiences were promised "the grandest, most realistic and overwhelmingly thrilling war-spectacle ever seen."

force the Sioux onto reservations. There he heard about the mortifying defeat of George Armstrong Custer's Seventh Cavalry at Little Bighorn, and he found himself engaged, a few days afterward, in a battle that was to become an inadvertent although electrifying real-life publicity stunt — a duel to the death with a young Cheyenne chieftain named Yellow Hair.

There were several versions of this confrontation, but the one that counted with the public sounded as if it were a chivalric tale from the Middle Ages, with Buffalo Bill in the role of the heroic knight. Yellow Hair, who was riding with a band of Cheyenne horsemen, spotted Cody with a detachment of the Fifth Cavalry and rode forth alone. "I know you, Pahaska," the chief yelled, addressing Cody by his Indian name, which meant Long Hair. "If you want to fight, come out and fight with me!"

The two champions spurred toward each other across the hundred yards of ground that separated their followers. Cody fired from the saddle and killed the Indian's horse just as his own mount stepped into a hole and went down. Both men fired again, this time at point-blank range. Yellow Hair toppled. Cody leaped upon him, stabbed him to the heart, wrenched off his war bonnet, sliced away at his scalp and then, standing up and waving the gory trophy, yelled, "First scalp for Custer."

Louisa Cody, now installed at Rochester, New York, was less than impressed by this feat of arms. Cody boxed up the scalp and sent it to her as a memento, one that grew increasingly odoriferous en route. She fainted (or claimed that she fainted) when she opened the package.

Unlike Louisa, however, the great American public was enthralled by this derring-do. Buffalo Bill's duel with Yellow Hand, as Yellow Hair's name was at first mistranslated, became instant folklore. Press Agent Burke hired a hack to write a new play, *The Red Right Hand, or Buffalo Bill's First Scalp For Custer,* and Cody — who had thoughtfully preserved Yellow Hair's effects for display on the road, and just as thoughtfully had wired the *New York Herald* an account of the fight — was back east again in the autumn of 1876 capitalizing on his adventure at the box office. He toured in Western melodramas for the next six years. But all this was simply prelude. Buffalo Bill, who

felt confined by ordinary theaters, was born, as events were to prove, for the hippodrome.

Cody had been toying for years with the idea of an outdoor show with real Indians, real buffalo and real cowboys on real horses. So had a manager-playwright-producer named Nate Salsbury, an imaginative man and a master of the logistics of big theatrical enterprises. Salsbury broached the idea during lunch with Buffalo Bill at a Brooklyn restaurant early in 1882, but wanted to postpone any such venture until he had researched the market and accumulated sufficient capital. Cody, less patient, had been invited to organize a Fourth of July "Old Glory Blowout" for the town of North Platte, Nebraska, and he now decided to experiment with a simulated buffalo hunt and a sharpshooting exhibition in addition to the bronc busting contests usual on such occasions.

The Blowout was a smashing success, so in the following year, 1883, Cody organized an outdoor show that included cowboys and Indians and elements of his Western melodramas, and took it on the road as The Wild West, Rocky Mountain and Prairie Exhibition. "The Grassy Sward Our Carpet," proclaimed the posters, "Heaven's Azure Canopy Our Canvas, No Gilding, No Humbug, No Freaks."

Cody was, in many ways, the ultimate showman, but he had neither the talent nor the temperament needed to feed, transport and exhibit an incongruous and restive collection of wild animals and hard-bitten men. He was totally unable to cope with the exhibition's catch-as-catch-can financing. Worse, he could not abide his partner in the enterprise, Dr. William F. Carver, a dentist turned trick-shot artist who billed himself as "The Evil Spirit of the Plains" and had invested $27,000 in the show. Cody got drunk and stayed drunk and the exhibition, although it drew large crowds, barely covered its overhead. After playing its way east to a five-week stand at Coney Island, it limped back to Omaha, where Cody and Carver parted company in anger and divided up the physical assets of the show.

Carver went on to tour the Southern United States with his own version of the Wild West, but plagued Cody with retaliatory lawsuits for years. Nate Salsbury, who had refused to share in any endeavor that involved the Evil Spirit of the Plains, stepped in to

rescue Buffalo Bill's show as its new producer. This took a great deal of doing. He found Cody drunk and lurching about in a plug hat amid "a gaping gang of bloodsuckers" before opening day the next year. Salsbury's remonstrations were in vain until the star's "liver flopped"—as Cody put it—in Pittsburgh, finally forcing him into reluctant sobriety. Bad weather left the enterprise $100,000 in the hole following a tour of the East, and most of the show's animals and equipment sank with a leaky Mississippi River steamboat that winter, during an invasion of the South.

But Salsbury found more money, and Cody, who could shun liquor when rising to an occasion, rounded up new buffalo, new cow ponies and new bucking broncs. It was a while before the show made a profit, but it was a theatrical success. Dazzled Eastern audiences, accustomed though they were to a rich diet of Western potboilers, seized on the exhibition as their first taste of the real thing, and it more than lived up to their inflated expectations. Buffalo Bill's Wild West, as it was now called—Cody never referred to it as a "show"—was authentic in many details, but it had about the same relationship to the true frontier as his own extraordinary career did to the prosaic experiences of the average Westerner.

His cowboys were indeed real cowboys, but in their spotless ten-gallon hats, furry chaps and gleaming spurs, they bore scant resemblance to the average sweat-stained ranch hands. Their skillful stock handling was presented as "Cowboy Fun," which caused wide-eyed dudes to conclude that life on the range was a day-to-day festival of rope tricks and bronc busting. His Indians were indeed real Indians, but he presented only the most flamboyant examples—usually mounted Sioux who appeared with fiercely painted faces and gaudy, feathered war bonnets. Drably dressed tribesmen were not recruited. And the Western scenes that he restaged—attacks on wagon trains or the Deadwood Mail (an actual coach from that Dakota Territory route: "the most famed vehicle extant") all ended happily, with the Indians repulsed decisively by Buffalo Bill and his cowboy pards.

Nate Salsbury's advertising made the most of Cody's passion for authenticity: "The Romantic West Brought East in Reality. Each Scene Instructive. A Year's Visit West in Three Hours." The spectators at these events were encouraged to believe that they were being educated as well as entertained as they cheered for the cavalry, jeered at the Indians and whooped in response to the Cowboy Band. They were convinced that they were in the presence of history when Cody galloped dramatically into the arena aboard his prancing white charger.

The troupe set forth with new optimism in 1885—having profited by its first year of seasoning—with a pair of new attractions that would prove impossible for most Americans to resist: Little Annie Oakley, a female sharpshooter who could split the edge of a playing card at 30 paces, and Sitting Bull, the Sioux chieftain who had assisted Custer to his doom.

Little Annie—real name Phoebe Anne Mozee—had begun demonstrating her genius with firearms as a child of nine by shooting the heads off running squirrels to help feed her impoverished Quaker family in Darke County, Ohio. She had beaten professional marksmen during her early teens (one of them, Frank Butler, later became her husband). She was 25 when she joined Cody's Wild West as "Little Sure Shot, a Wonder of the Age" and she could do things with guns that defied understanding. She reduced spectators to awe with one spectacular feat: breaking a small glass ball, which was whirled on the end of a string by her husband, while sighting into a mirror and shooting backward over her shoulder. She was a tiny thing—just five feet tall—and she looked even smaller decked out in the cowboy hat, medal-bedecked blouse and short, pleated skirt that she wore in the arena. She responded to applause with a warm and eager smile, and performed her noisy miracles with an ease and innocence that delighted and enslaved her audiences.

No one was more captivated than Sitting Bull, who was so carried away by her facility with guns that he adopted her as his daughter and watched her every performance with unflagging admiration and astonishment. The old chief led a curious life with the show, which he served, mostly, as a kind of living, breathing waxworks exhibit—a role he had accepted to escape the boredom of life on a reservation, and to provide for two wives and 11 children who relied on him for support. He bargained, however, before signing on. He had a weakness for oyster stew and hard candy and talked the show's management into providing him with

Employing techniques and utensils suitable for an army, cooks prepare a meal for hundreds of Wild West performers and hands.

Show managers, including treasurer Jule Keen (*second from right*) and publicist John Burke (*right*), idle before the treasury tent.

both, as well as $50 a week and the sole right to sell photographs of himself.

Crowds booed Sitting Bull a good deal when he sat on his horse in the arena, though rubbernecks took no such liberties when they peered nervously into his tent between shows. He was displeased by the booing, but did not hold a grudge. He was appalled to discover that the white man let homeless waifs drift about the streets of big cities, and he gave much of his pay away to newsboys and other urchins he encountered on the tour.

Annie and Sitting Bull drew thousands to the box office, but the show owed as much to Nate Salsbury, who brought it system, orderly performance and double-entry bookkeeping. Buffalo Bill's Wild West moved across country on a snow-white, 26-car special train, which its roustabouts loaded and unloaded with efficiency and dispatch. The show had vast canvas backdrops depicting the Wyoming Rockies, and its own lighting system for night performances. The faithful John Burke was freed to invent new exercises in ballyhoo: he invited the public to wander through the show's camping grounds, and held "Indian rib roasts" at which dignitaries crouched around fires gnawing meat impaled on sharpened sticks. And the paying customers poured in. Cody was delighted with the "thousands of expectant countenances" he saw every time he entered the arena. It was, he said, a sight "to make a man a laughing hyena with happiness."

The show made $100,000 in 1885 and did far better the following season, when it drew a million people during its run on Staten Island and another million during a winter stand in Madison Square Garden. The latter featured "Custer's Massacre," with Cody standing head bowed in a spotlight on the darkened battlefield while the legend "TOO LATE" was projected onto a screen. Mrs. Custer attended; so did Henry Ward Beecher, P. T. Barnum, August Belmont and General William Tecumseh Sherman. Mark Twain was delighted: "Genuine . . . down to its smallest details. It is often said that none of the exhibitions we send to England are purely and distinctly American. If you will take the Wild West Show over there you can remove that reproach." The show took Twain's advice and sailed aboard the steamship *State of Nebraska* in the spring of 1887 to help the English to celebrate Queen Victoria's Golden Jubilee. ◉

On the back lot between staged massacres, Wild West show Indians try out a new white man's game, table tennis. They wear full ceremonial costume in readiness for their next cue to return to the arena.

Packaging the white man's goods in Indian appeal

Wild West show impresarios were not the first sharp-eyed businessmen to recognize the commercial value of the Indian. Patent-medicine hucksters had long exploited the exotic aura of the Indian and the ignorance of customers by peddling nostrums purportedly concocted to the recipe of a celebrated medicine man. A few pitchmen even devised circus-like Indian medicine shows, forerunners of the extravaganzas of Buffalo Bill and his competitors.

The success of Wild West shows made it clear that the romantic appeal of the Indian could sell more than just noxious cure-alls. In the late 19th and early 20th Centuries, Indian names and faces appeared on vendibles from soap to automobiles. In a few cases, like tobacco, the product might have had some connection with the American Indian, but it is unlikely that any Indians of the era shared in the profits of the items their images helped to sell.

Seminude Indian women were a favored motif in barroom advertising like this beer-tray picture.

The Indian on this wrapper lends his air of nobility to the soap's claim to purity.

A stern-faced warrior and his weapons embellish this sticker for an orange crate.

A fanciful "Indian Queen" collects the essence of a flower on this perfume label.

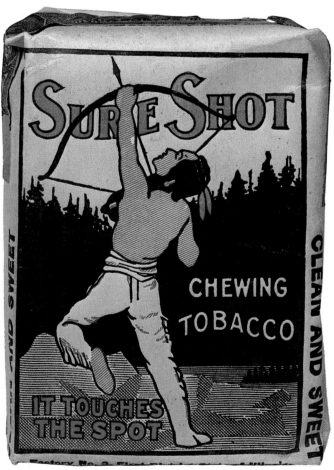

An Indian bowman on the packet offers metaphorical assurance of the efficacy of this brand of chewing tobacco.

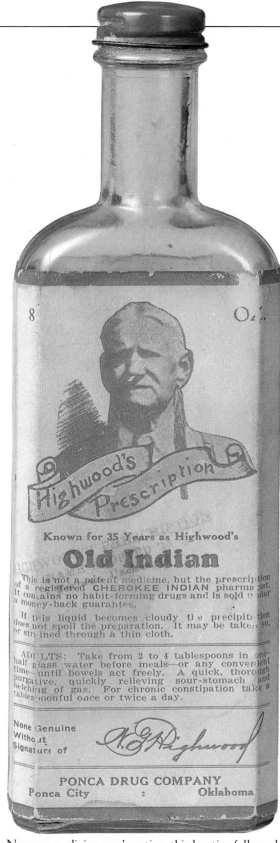

No mere medicine man's potion, this laxative followed the "prescription of a registered Cherokee pharmacist."

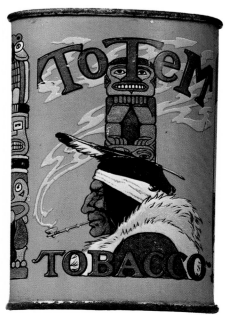

A happy Indian enjoys this early product of the tobacco giant P. Lorillard Company.

Orcico, an acronym for Orrison Cigar Company, sounded like an Indian name and inspired the container's artwork.

The cough drops in this container were purported to include the same herbs that Indians used to treat sore throats.

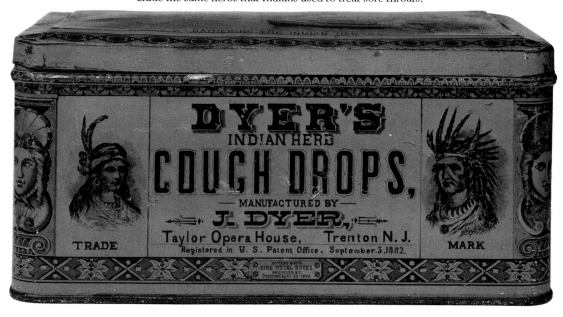

seurs and English lancers brought back from Europe to augment its cowboys and Indians.

But Buffalo Bill was always short of cash. He wrote piteously to Salsbury for a $5,000 loan in January 1895, promising to "sell everything to pay you if we fail to make money next summer." He could not resist requests for handouts, particularly those broached by pretty, compliant young women. He spent $80,000 backing plays in England and New York for Katherine Clemmons, a beautiful British actress, before fleeing her increasingly expensive company, declaring, "I'd rather manage a million Indians than one soubrette." He bought a printing plant for one Hugh Wetmore, a newspaperman who married Cody's sister Helen— and was repaid with a poem that began, " 'I know ye Long Hair,' yells Yellow Hand/A-ridin out from his pesky band." He showered money on his daughters, Irma and Arta, and for Louisa he built a big house outside North Platte, calling it Welcome Wigwam.

Nor could he resist get-rich-quick schemes. "In his business dealings he was like a child," said Gordon Lillie, a latter-day business associate. Cody thought of money only when he needed to spend it, said Lillie, "then, if he did not have it or could not borrow it, he became sick—actually sick so that he would have to go to bed." He financed a promoter bent on colonizing plots of Mexican real estate, and another who produced White Beaver Cough Cream and Great Lung Healer.

But such minor expenditures were dwarfed by the extravagances into which Buffalo Bill plunged for the purpose—or so he thought—of increasing his wealth and achieving a dignity to match that of the rich Americans and titled foreigners with whom he drank and hobnobbed as a performer. He became a victim, over the years, of his own grandiose ambitions and his own enormous optimism, though a good many of his larger ideas were sound enough in themselves. He invested in land and blooded cattle, and his 4,000-acre Scout's Rest Ranch was a showplace of western Nebraska in the 1890s—as, indeed, it should have been, since he spent a great deal more on a 12-mile irrigation ditch and on the 80 horses and 40 men he kept at work on the place than it ever seems to have made in profits.

But this was a small matter to a man of such imperial designs; as the money poured in, he poured it out to acquire 400,000 more acres in Wyoming's Big Horn Basin, to construct the Cody Canal to bring water into a vast irrigation system, to snap up and stock peripheral grazing land (the TE Ranch, the Irma Lake Ranch, Sweeney Ranch, Rock Creek Ranch) and to found Cody, Wyoming, complete with an Irma Hotel and a newspaper, *The Cody Enterprise.* He built himself a hunting lodge, Pahaska Tepee. He persuaded the Burlington Railroad to build a branch line into Cody and the government to spend $50,000 on a stagecoach road from nearby Yellowstone National Park. "My good friend Buffalo Bill has hit the trail up there," said Teddy Roosevelt, "and I would take a chance on building a road into eternity on his statement."

Few settlers arrived on the Burlington's trains, however, despite Cody's claims of loam 21 feet deep. His irrigation scheme bogged down in financial disaster. The citizenry of Cody had to pay 25 cents a barrel for water hauled by wagon from the Shoshone River until the government stepped in and saved the town with its own water reclamation project. Few visitors used the road into Yellowstone Park and the Irma Hotel went $500 deeper into debt with every passing month.

These drains on capital were ruinously compounded when Buffalo Bill plunged into a mining venture that he hoped would make him rich as an Oriental potentate overnight. Colonel D. B. Dyer, a former Indian agent, told him that fresh riches in gold, tungsten and lead could be extracted from an exhausted copper mine, the Campo Bonito, near the town of Oracle in Arizona's Catalina Mountains. Cody joined Dyer in founding the Cody-Dyer Mining and Milling Company, put up money for wagon roads and an ore-crushing mill, and in the next dozen years let Dyer fleece him of $500,000 by padding payrolls and falsifying bills while sending him glowing reports of bonanzas soon to come.

There were reasons, beyond those rooted in his native optimism, for Cody's willingness to believe in these promises of sudden wealth. He not only hoped to solve the financial dilemmas in which he had engulfed himself in the Big Horn Basin, but to escape the increase drudgery of life in the arena. Nate Salsbury fell ill in 1894 and James A. Bailey of Barnum and Bailey's Circus took over management of the Wild West. Bailey booked the show into a wearying succession of one-, two- and three-night stands—132 of them in 1896. Cody was growing older, his hair was thinning,

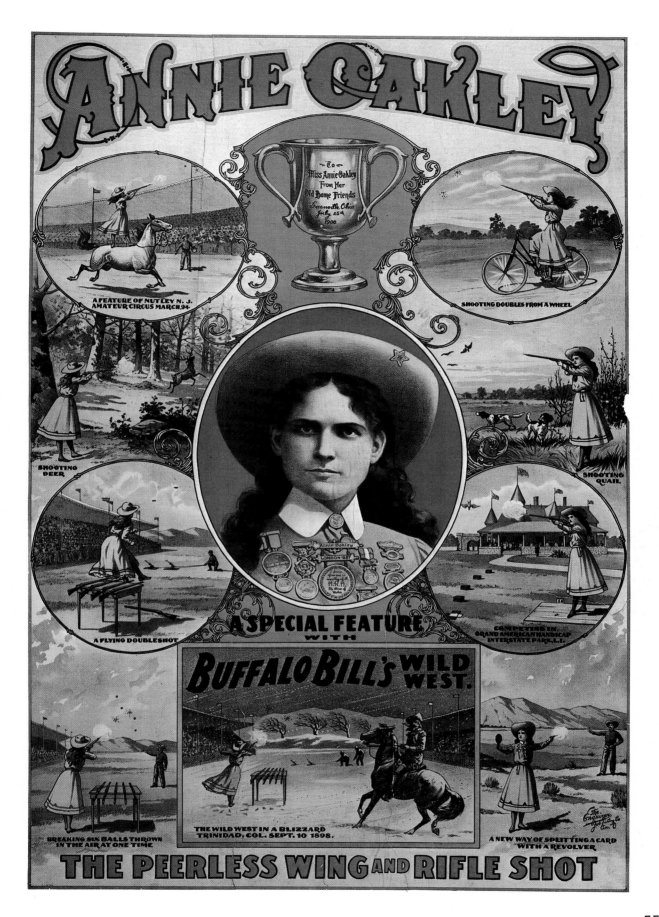

his years of drinking had begun to sap his enormous vitality and he yearned, in moments of despondency, for retirement and a new and more satisfying life.

In preparation, in the early 1900s, he decided to shuck off Louisa, perhaps to settle down with a more compatible woman. Louisa (or Lulu, as he called her) had taken a dim view of Cody's enterprises from the time of the Golden Rule Hotel, and of his morals since she had found him kissing a knot of actresses after an 1877 Omaha show. Cody stayed away as much as possible, and usually got protectively drunk before calling on her at the Welcome Wigwam. But he endured her harangues as he had once endured dust storms, and tried to compensate for his failings by showering her with money. "I often feel sorry for her," he wrote from England to a man who cut Lulu's lawn. "If she gets cranky just laugh at it, she can't help it."

He began changing his mind, however, when the Waldorf-Astoria sent him a bill for mirrors, vases and furniture Lulu smashed up in a tantrum in 1898. (She had arrived unexpectedly in New York and another woman had answered when she telephoned Cody's room at the Hoffman House.) "I have tried & tried to think that it was right for me to go on through all my life living a false lie," he wrote his sister Julia, "just because I was too much of a Morral coward to do otherwise. But my married life grows more unbearable each year. Divorces are not looked down upon as they used to be—people are getting more enlightened. They say it's better than living a life of misery for both. God did not intend joining two persons together for both to go through life miserable.

"When such a mistake was made—A law was created to undo the mistake. As it is I have no future to look forward to—no happiness. Lulu will be better contented. She will be her absolute master—I will give her every bit of the North Platte property. And an annual income. If she will give me a quiet legal separation—if she won't do this then it's war and publicity." Lulu refused to cooperate; Cody claimed she tried to poison him after he arrived at the Welcome Wigwam, drunk, during the Christmas holidays in 1900 and collapsed while eating. He sued her for divorce, only to find her harder to escape than debt and hangovers.

Lulu made herself an object of sympathy during the divorce trial in Wyoming, and counteracted a good

Frontier fever in Bavaria

Germans thronged to Buffalo Bill's shows—and they lost none of their enthusiasm for the Wild West after the troupe departed. For years they had followed the imaginary exploits of Old Shatterhand, the frontiersman hero of the German pulp writer Karl May. Now they formed organizations in which to act out their own frontier fantasies. Wild West clubs arose in practically every major German city.

Less concerned with the bloodthirsty heroics of gunfighters than with the everyday lore of the West, members studied Western history, collected books and artifacts, and each one adopted the name and identity of a Western figure. "Indians" tried to master ceremonial songs and dances while "cowboys" concentrated on fancy riding and roping—all to prepare for the clubs' Wild West shows, where each member could play his chosen role before admiring audiences.

A broncobuster decorates the official calling card of the South Munich club. The card notes that the Cowboy Club was founded in 1913; it met, appropriately, in a saloon.

At the Munich club's Wild West show in 1928, a burgher sports a headdress and tomahawk along with his Bavarian vest and chain.

After his performance at a club function in 1933, White Eagle, a genuine Sioux Indian, gets his beer *humpen* refilled by a man in full Bavarian costume. White Eagle reportedly went to Munich as a student and stayed to earn his living singing in taverns.

On horses borrowed from a local riding academy, "Indians" from the Cowboy Club entertain onlookers as they follow a wagonload of "cowboys" past Munich's city hall in a parade during Fasching, the German pre-Lenten festival, in 1928.

Storefronts in Washington, Iowa, are plastered with ads for a 1909 performance of Cody's and Pawnee Bill's show. The result of their 1908 partnership was known to employees as the "Two Bills Show."

The two Wild West impresarios strike regal postures in this nine-foot poster of 1910. The high cost of such advertising did the merger in when a printing company foreclosed a $66,000 debt in 1913.

many of Cody's witnesses by the mild and injured air she wore when testifying. "Will," she told the court, "is one of the kindest and most generous men I ever knew. When he was sober he was gentle and considerate. If I had him to myself now there would be no trouble. His environments have caused him to put this upon me." Their daughter Arta had only recently died in Spokane—of a broken heart, claimed Lulu, because her father was insisting on divorce.

The plaintiff produced witnesses who painted a different picture. Mrs. John Boyer, whose husband ran the Scout's Rest Ranch, stated that Cody had been rendered unconscious at Christmas because Lulu had sneaked a gypsy love potion called Dragon's Blood into his coffee. And a Mrs. H. S. Parker testified that Lulu was so jealous that she suspected Queen Victoria of having a romantic interest in her husband. The judge had this last tidbit stricken, hurriedly, from the record but Lulu made capital of the Christmas potion: she *had* adulterated his coffee with an aphrodisiac in an attempt to recapture his affection, but the drug was also calcu-

lated to cure him of his awful desire for strong drink, surely a commendable aim for a good wife. As for the charge that she refused "to go anywhere with that old reprobate," she had pleaded to join her husband in Europe, but had been turned down on grounds of expense while he spent fortunes on Katherine Clemmons. "But I suppose Will wants a young wife. . . ."

Cody's case was dismissed, and he glumly paid his wife's court costs of $318. He had reason for bitterness. Lulu had been both grasping and abusive outside the courtroom; she had filed her countersuit after accepting the North Platte property with which he had thought to achieve a separation and had threatened to denounce him at their daughter's grave. But he nevertheless turned back to her—his familiar enemy, his companion in misery—as time went on. He was growing used to the unkindness of fate and becoming aware that his gaudy enterprises were to be the burdens rather than the salvation of his old age.

Buffalo Bill and his Wild West could still draw crowds—astonishingly so for attractions that had al-

This rare poster—cut into pieces to fit the scrapbook of a collector of the era—was issued after Buffalo Bill's final appearance and thus was the only "Last Performance" notice that could be believed. Six years of shows, each advertised as Cody's last, passed between his first "farewell speech" in 1910 and his actual last bow in 1916.

Buffalo Bill, Col. Joseph C. Miller & Chief Wa-Na-Sa-Ga
*Leaving the Show after the Afternoon Performance,
Closing date, Norfolk, Va. The Performance that
marked the end of COL. CODY'S 40 Years of
Circus Life.*

ready toured the world for so many years—and the show staged a final tour of Europe in 1906 with its famed spectacles: *Le Dernier Combat du General Custer* and *Attaque du Dead Wood Mail Coach*. It drew big crowds in Marseilles but some of its potential audience was siphoned off thereafter by a fly-by-night competitor, J. T. McCaddon's International Shows, which included both a circus and a Wild West exhibition. Cody's show lost 200 of its 300 horses to an

equine disease called glanders and his new manager and partner, James Bailey, died. Worse yet, Bailey's family acquired Cody's interest in the show by foreclosing on a debt he owed his deceased partner. The show was sold two years later, in 1908, to Gordon Lillie, a fellow entrepreneur who billed himself as Pawnee Bill.

Cody, now in his 60s, was tired, paunchy and subject to a new embarrassment: the need to wear a hairpiece in the arena to cover his thinning white locks. He was mortified, after lifting his hat on one occasion, to realize that he had removed his hairpiece. His weariness and discouragement were intensified by the fact that he did not own even a share of the enterprise. But Lillie, shrewdly aware that the show was worth little without Buffalo Bill, gave him back a half interest and, in effect, a last chance at some kind of financial recovery. The Wild West (with Pawnee Bill's Great Far East) hit the road in 1910 behind advance billing that made Cody irresistible to all who had ever seen him. Audiences sat in deathly quiet and many wept when he rode into a spotlight on his white horse and told them: "This farewell visit will be my last 'Hail and farewell' in the saddle to you all. . . .

"I am about to go home for a well earned rest. Out in the West I have my horses, my buffaloes, my sturdy, staunch old Indian friends—my home and my green fields. I want to see nature in its prime and to enjoy a rest from active life. My message to you tonight is one of farewell. Thirty years ago you gave me my first welcome. I am grateful for your loyal devotion to me. During that time many of my friends among you and many of those with me have been long since gathered to the great, unknown arena of another life—there are only a few of us left. When I went away from here each year before I merely said goodnight—this time it will mean goodbye. To my little friends in the gallery, and the grownups who used to sit there, I thank you once again. God bless you all—goodbye."

Cody meant it; but fate, the Arizona mine and one Harry H. Tammen had a more lugubrious future in store for him. He was flat broke three years later—though he had gone through the embarrassing business of saying goodbye all over again in 1911 and 1912 and had sold the Scout's Rest Ranch at a loss—and he was delighted when Tammen, co-owner of *The Denver Post,* offered to loan him $20,000 for six months to put some cash in his pockets again.

This turned out to be the most demoralizing of his financial misadventures. Tammen, a jolly fellow, was a sharper of marvelous unscrupulousness. He had acquired a dog-and-pony show he renamed the Sells Floto Circus, and had decided that Buffalo Bill was just the attraction it needed to become a profitable enterprise. He used the $20,000 note as a lien on the Wild West, put it out of business through a series of Byzan-

tine legal maneuvers, and forced Cody into a demeaning vassalage that was to claim him even in the grave.

Buffalo Bill's first venture with Tammen, in the fall of 1913, was tolerable for the old scout. Cody played himself in a movie *(page 204)* that re-created some of his past adventures, including his duel with Yellow Hair. The films were shown in nickelodeons, but did not earn enough to pay off Cody's debt to Tammen, and in early 1914 Buffalo Bill joined the Sells Floto Circus. Cody was never braver than in the 36 awful months that followed. He was sick with rheumatism, neuritis and an inflamed prostate when he hit the road with Tammen's sleazy tent show in hopes of paying his way to freedom. He aggravated these ailments with whiskey, which, having signed a pledge limiting himself to three drinks a day, he sipped from beer steins. He did not complain, though he was often so weak that he had to enter in a buggy rather than on horseback.

But he was finally moved to rebellion, for all that. "This man," he wrote to a friend, "is driving me crazy. Won't someone who knows the law come to my rescue? I avoided killing in the bad days. I don't want to kill him. But if there is no justice left, I will." He sat down with Tammen in Lawrence, Kansas, toward the end of his second year, put two loaded pistols on the table, announced that he considered his debts paid and that he was quitting Sells Floto at the end of the tour. Tammen threatened lawsuits against him, but was moved to discretion as he noticed his victim's shaky old hand sliding occasionally in the direction of a six-shooter, and eventually acquiesced.

Cody was capable, even in his beleaguered dotage, of marvelous recoveries from affliction and despondency. He finished his second year with Sells Floto in a state of complete physical collapse (the show's schedule having called for 366 performances in 183 days along a route of 16,878 miles) but rose in a couple of weeks to shoot deer in Wyoming. He talked grandly, on escaping Tammen, of new money-making schemes and sold his services, for cash advances calculated to further these ambitions, to another show, the Miller Brothers and Arlington 101 Ranch Wild West. But only courage and a recurring delusion—"I am climbing toward another fortune"—sustained him after the show went on the road; uremic poisoning provoked a deterioration of his kidneys and heart in the summer of

1916 and he could not sit on a horse without agony from his ailing prostate.

A one-time Wild West sharpshooter, Johnny Baker, hoisted him into the saddle each night and watched him carefully as he slumped there, chin on chest, eyes closed, awaiting his cue. Cody was afraid of "dying before all those people in the arena," but he straightened every time the curtains opened, spurred into the lights and applause as Baker said, "Ready, Colonel," and kept his chin up and his hat held high until the horse brought him back into the shadows to slide, groaning, to the ground. He hung on, somehow, until the final performance at Portsmouth, Virginia, in November of 1916, and then he forced himself back across the country to Wyoming for a dinner that was to be given in his honor at the Irma Hotel in Cody. But he had ridden his last white charger.

He went to a Colorado sanitarium to take a mineral-water cure, but the attending medicine man, a Dr. W. W. Crook, told the newspapers, "There is no hope, whatever," and shipped Cody to Denver and a bed at the home of his sister, Mrs. May Decker. Lulu, his remaining daughter Irma, and another sister were summoned and a Dr. East called in. The new physician, a man apparently given to lively diagnostic thinking, explained that the old scout's condition was being worsened by an eclipse of the moon. Cody seemed uninterested in cause, as the doctor reported to newspapermen on leaving him, but demanded to know the details of effect. What, he asked, were his chances?

"There is a time," said East, "when the physician must commend his patient to a higher power."

"How long?" asked Cody.

"The sand is slipping slowly...." East told him, but Cody interrupted: "How *long,* doctor?"

"About thirty-six hours, sir."

"All right," said Buffalo Bill, and called in Lew Decker, his brother-in-law. "The doc says I've got thirty-six hours. Let's play some cards." He seemed as unconcerned to those who called to say goodbye. "It was the last handshake," said Chauncey Thomas, an old friend. "I knew it; he knew it, but on the surface not a sign." Cody died at 12:05 p.m. on January 10, 1917, with as little fuss as concern — but not without inspiring headlines from coast to coast and a final round of applause, led by President Woodrow Wilson with a

message of condolence from the White House. Teddy Roosevelt hastened to describe him as "an American of Americans," and governors, clergymen and other dignitaries lent themselves to similar encomiums. General Nelson A. Miles, for whom Cody had scouted during the Indian wars, called him "a high minded gentleman whose exploits will live forever."

Denver Post reporter Gene Fowler — later a famous biographer — was more vivid: "Indiscreet, prodigal, temperamental as a diva, pompous but naïve, vain but generous, bigger than big today, littler than little tomorrow, Cody lived with the world at his feet and died with it on his shoulders." Fowler spoke with a certain authority. Cody had not escaped Harry H. Tammen by dying and Fowler was to act as the instrument of the publisher's gaudy promotional instincts once his fellow citizens were finished ushering the old scout toward his grave.

This was not a modest process. The Colorado legislature decreed that Cody's body lie in state in the rotunda of the state capitol; a crowd of 25,000 passed by the bier while a master of ceremonies in a silk hat urged, "Step lively, folks ... big crowd behind." Infan-

rock to keep promoters from North Platte, Cody or Omaha from stealing the body.

Any elements of bad taste still unexploited materialized as if by magic when Buffalo Bill was conducted, at last, to his final resting place. Sells Floto wagons were interspersed among the 3,000 automobiles that clanked and steamed up the mountain road on the day of the rites; the more raffish among the crowd tilted whiskey bottles at the grave site; artillerymen fired an 11-gun salute; and six of Cody's old girl friends arranged themselves on camp stools by his bronze casket and stole the show from Lulu, while speeches, as Fowler put it, "were made by expert liars."

Still, there was a certain inevitability, even a kind of fitness, about it all. The hubbub surrounding Buffalo Bill's death was no more outlandish than the many exaggerations of his life. For half a century—ever since he had first shaken Ned Buntline's hand—his image had been so distorted by dime novelists and press agents that his achievements as a plainsman had long since been buried beneath a mountain of hyperbole. But his greatest achievement was his enormous impact on the public consciousness, and that lived on.

Buffalo Bill was one of the prime creators of the West that survives in the imagination of America and the world. His show distilled the vast and untidy American frontier into a bright handful of symbols that became indestructible stock metaphors for almost all who made art or entertainment of Western themes thereafter. The fierce, painted Indian and the daredevil cowboy, the imperiled stagecoach and the encircled wagon train represented the West not only to his contemporaries, but to hundreds of millions who later would encounter the same icons in popular fiction and on movie and television screens around the world.

But Cody's influence was due to more than his skill as a packager of Western images. His effectiveness stemmed from his ability to transmit his own boyish enthusiasm for the frontier. He was an entrepreneur who believed passionately in his product, and he spent his entire life selling a romantic version of the West that was based on his own genuinely exciting career as an Indian-fighter, Army scout and all-purpose plainsman. He made the West seem exceptionally glamorous because that was how he saw it. It is still difficult, because of him, to believe that it was ever any other way.

try and a regimental band from Fort Logan led a funeral parade, with Buffalo Bill's last white horse, McKinley, following the hearse bearing an empty saddle. Boy Scouts, Elks, Knights Templar, Civil and Spanish-American War veterans, Shriners and members of the Showman's League of America fell in behind. Cody had been a member of the Elks and the funeral service was held at Denver Lodge, No. 17, B.P.O.E., where a quartet sang "Tenting Tonight on the Old Camp Ground." But Cody's corpse was then transported to Olinger's mortuary to await further arrangements.

Now Tammen and Fowler took over. The old scout had asked to be buried on Cedar Mountain above Cody, Wyoming, and had drawn a will directing that $10,000 be used to place him there. But some friends said he also had expressed a wish to be interred atop Lookout Mountain, just west of Denver. Tammen lobbied for the latter grave site for the greater glory of Denver, the *Post,* and the Sells Floto Circus, and Lulu gave that choice her blessing—Cody having failed to leave the $10,000 to implement the Cedar Mountain plan. Actual burial was delayed for five months, during which Tammen contrived a steel vault in the mountain

Ropers, riders and chorus girls

Wild West shows, first conceived by Buffalo Bill, survived him only fitfully. Within three months of his death, America had entered World War I and turned its attention to global heroics. By 1918 there were no major Wild West shows on the road. The few after the War were a new breed— displays of cowboy skills with circus and vaudeville acts. The frontier pageantry that had been the backbone of Cody's show disappeared from the arena, although it was quickly appropriated by the infant movie industry.

The Miller Brothers 101 Ranch Wild West was typical of the post-war shows. It had first been launched in 1908, a by-product of a fabulous 110,000-acre Oklahoma ranch empire owned by three brothers named Miller. Using their own cowhands for much of the talent, the Millers built their show around displays of trick riding, roping and shooting. The performers—among them Tom Mix, Buck Jones and Mabel Normand, all later silent-film stars—rotated between the show and the ranch, which served as a kind of Wild West training ground.

The Millers spent the war years raising livestock for the government. When the show reopened in 1925, it included ballet dancers, Ziegfield girls and trained elephants but was still billed as "Real Wild West." It was, at least, more real than its handful of competitors, most of which were simply appendages to circuses and carnivals. By 1931, when the Miller show went bankrupt, even its mainstay ranch-life acts had been upstaged by the newly popular competitive rodeos.

Leaning against a barn covered with 101 Ranch posters, three Oklahoma boys read pamphlets promoting the show. The horses, Longhorns and Hampshire hogs on the posters were products of the ranch, one of the largest diversified farms in America.

3 | Off the range and into the arena

One of the most enduring images of the West is that of a cowboy riding on a wild, bucking horse. The era it commemorates—when longhorn steers were driven across the plains by men mounted on horses they first had to break—was brief. Yet the spirit of the rugged cowboy has persisted like a champion rider glued to the saddle. One reason has been the rodeo.

The founders of modern rodeo observed the ways of the cowboy fading "like the dissolving views of memory," as the organizers of the first Frontier Days in Cheyenne, Wyoming, put it. To keep the memory—and part of the reality—alive, they brought the West of the cowboy into the arena.

The men who had tamed wild horses and roped and branded cattle as everyday tasks eventually were succeeded by the cavaliers of sport who performed for glory and prizes. However, the jobs of rodeo performers—whether riding bucking broncs, wrestling with frantic steers or clinging to the backs of mean-spirited bulls—required as much hard work and were just as punishing and dangerous as the jobs of their cowboy ancestors.

As a wrangler yanks off the blindfold, a bronco explodes and the rider hangs on with championship style during this event in 1918.

While a mounted assistant prevents the animal from turning, a rodeo cowboy leaps onto a running steer before wrestling it to the ground. This event is often called bulldogging because some early performers stopped steers by sinking their teeth—bulldog-style—into the beasts' lips.

93

A steer does a sudden backflip as a roper turns his horse into a wrenching stop. Frequent injury to steers when they were thus "busted" caused many states to prohibit steer-roping in the 1920s, while others allowed the practice to continue under strict rules that protected the cattle.

95

A hapless cowboy and a viciously bucking Brahma bull part company during a rodeo in 1946. One novice bull rider, after he had tangled with what he described as a "ton-and-a-half black brute," said that the experience was similar to having his spine slammed together like an accordion.

97

The rodeo: a legacy of challenge, chance and courage

There is no telling when the first rodeo took place. One legend says it occurred at Deer Trail, Colorado Territory, some time in the late 1860s. The contestants were cowhands of the Hashknife, Camp Stool and Mill Iron Ranches who matched their toughest horses against their toughest men during a respite taken when their herds converged on a trail drive. Other stories go further back, to the fiestas of the old Spanish West. One of these was described in 1847 by an American Army officer in a letter written from occupied Santa Fe during the Mexican War: "At this time of year the cowmen have what is called the round-up, when the calves are branded and the fat beasts selected to be driven to a fair hundreds of miles away. This round-up is a great time for the cowhands, a Donneybrook fair it is indeed. They contest with each other for the best roping and throwing, and there are horse races and whiskey and wines. At night in the clear moonlight there is much dancing in the streets."

Cowboys gathered to let off steam at similarly noisy and informal rites throughout the last decades of the 1800s—sometimes on coming into towns on holidays, sometimes on the open range when seeking respite from more mundane toil. There were few spectators other than the whooping contestants themselves and no financial rewards except those yielded by the kind of betting that such men could afford. But these rude contests were the beginnings of 20th Century public rodeo with its regulated events, carefully calculated prize systems and grandstands packed with fans hungering for a taste of the Old West.

Looking every ounce the big Western wheeler-dealer, C. B. Irwin greets a parade crowd with the enthusiasm that made him a successful promoter of early rodeos.

By the 1950s, when rodeo had become a major professional sport, the cattle country was long since fenced, the rough skills of the open range had given way to modern stock-handling science and the working ranch hand was as likely to be found punching cows from the seat of a pickup truck as from the back of a horse. Rodeo, rather than ranching, had inherited the danger, unpredictability and raw excitement that had once lured men to the cowpuncher's life.

Rodeo contestants were still called cowboys, but their skills had little in common with the kind of prosaic labor it took to bring beef to market. They could rope a calf, wrestle a steer to the ground, or stick to the back of a plunging horse or bull for eight explosive seconds, but few could have put these skills to more practical use. Some had scarcely encountered a horse or a cow outside the arena. Scandalized oldtimers grumbled that young stars who regularly picked up prize money for riding broncs could not handle a cow pony well enough to haze a stray calf back to its herd.

The rodeo cowboy reflected the spirit of the Old West more truly, nevertheless, than any other remnant of those headstrong and turbulent days. He was the same hard, hopeful breed of man as his rugged predecessors of the 19th Century: foot-loose, reckless, ruefully philosophical, contemptuous of pain and often taciturn (or even shy) in the presence of strangers. The necessities of his trade—hats, chaps, ropes and saddles—were the same tools the first American cattlemen of the Southwest had borrowed from the *vaqueros* of old Mexico. And the "short horse" he used for roping and steer wrestling was the quarter horse of the frontier— an animal that evolved before the range was fenced.

He had scant acquaintance, in many cases, with the gritty chores of ranching, but the rodeo cowboy was subjected to pressures the oldtime range rider never knew. He competed in as many shows as possible in

pursuit of prizes, and found himself not only submitting his body to constant abuse in competition, but traveling hundreds, even thousands of miles between arenas for months at a time. He paid for his own equipment, anted up entrance fees before every appearance and was judged for championships by that most pragmatic of standards: dollars earned. His was a solitary endeavor; no team physician interceded when he was hurt and he got no pension when time had eroded his skills.

The rodeo contestant clung stubbornly to this bruising, exhausting and often unrewarding way of life for exactly the reasons the mountain men, prospectors and line riders of the Old West clung to theirs: pride in his own hardihood, a kind of veiled contempt for stay-at-homes with regular jobs and regular lives, the hope of striking it rich and the stimulation of danger and suspense. Alone among all perpetuators of Western tradition he endured, deep into the 20th Century, as a replica of men who formed such traditions before the prairies were plowed and the open ranges enclosed.

Few realize how quickly civilization engulfed the great cattle kingdoms of the Old West. The era of open ranges lasted hardly more than 20 years after the end of the Civil War. By the 1880s the foot-loose cowboy of the long northbound trails found himself becoming a figure of the past, outmoded by the railroads that materialized throughout the cattle country and by fences thrown up across the routes longhorns had taken to Wichita and Abilene.

Homesteaders who followed the railroads took a far more sober view of life than the buckaroos they displaced, but they were fascinated by the cowboys' reckless exhibitions of skill, and they incorporated riding and roping contests into their civic celebrations almost from the first. These early Western festivals were known as "bucking shows" or "cowboy tournaments" and were held on the Fourth of July or other civic occasions in ball parks, fairgrounds, stockyards or even pastures on the outskirts of towns. Spectators in wagons and buggies and on foot encircled the scene of action and sometimes found themselves forced to dodge or to grab the bridles of their teams as maddened broncs or steers came plunging into their midst.

The organizers of one of the noisiest of these Fourth of July celebrations used the main street of Pecos, Texas, for a riding and roping contest between cowboys from various ranches in 1883. Although contes-

tants competed for prizes for the first time, spectators were able to watch the fun for nothing by simply gathering along the street. Admission fees were finally levied when citizens of Prescott, Arizona, staged a Fourth of July Frontier Days celebration in 1888. They not only proved that tickets could be sold without provoking civil disturbances, but discovered that rodeo audiences spent money in local stores and that such shows would inflate the reputation of the town that sponsored them. Businessmen in Cheyenne, Wyoming, and Pendleton, Oregon, carried these concepts further when they, too, began holding annual cowboy shows; they went to elaborate lengths to outdo each other with theatrical effects and with ballyhoo calculated to draw spectators from surrounding states.

Church bells were rung, locomotive whistles blown and cannon fired in neighboring Fort Russell to herald the opening of Cheyenne's first Frontier Days celebration in 1897. A great many citizens, charmed by this cacophony, hurried into the streets to loose off pistols, rifles and shotguns as well. Crowds filled the local fairgrounds to the bursting point and its fences were torn down when a thousand additional spectators advanced on the festivities from two special trains that arrived from Denver after the show had begun. The schedule of events included a bucking contest, six horse races and a steer-roping competition—which had to be canceled after the audience became unruly and crowded into the arena.

There were no complaints; there was too much else to watch. A battalion of infantry from Fort Russell marched into the infield, pitched its tents and engaged in a mock battle; a delegation of Oglala Sioux stalked into view in feathers and bells and stamped through a series of dances; and a dummy, dressed to approximate a captured outlaw, was strung up and riddled with bullets during a presentation entitled: "A Scene on the Overland Trail."

The big annual Western festival at Cheyenne grew increasingly eclectic as time wore on. Its promoters brought in acts from Wild West shows, set cowboys to roping wolves, and augmented performances in the arena with balloon ascensions, parachute drops, masquerade balls and street dances. Spectators were privileged, at some Frontier Days shows, to watch pioneer weddings—actual marriage ceremonies in which volunteer couples, decked out in Western costumes, were united in wedlock in front of the grandstand. Crowds

101

not only grew but responded to the festivities with a noisy, even riotous, enthusiasm that succeeding audiences felt duty bound to emulate. One stupefied out-of-town spectator, Dr. Jeremiah Meyer of Toledo, Ohio, spoke for thousands of visitors when he said: "I am a surgeon in a State Insane Asylum, and used to excitement, but Cheyenne takes the cake."

The Pendleton Round-Up, inaugurated in 1910, offered similarly gaudy pageantry. Author Charles Furlong recalled one hair-raising event in his book, *Let 'Er Buck:* a "maverick race" in which 30 cowboys tried to rope one maddened steer while riding in "a smother of dust." There were Indian races in which each rider was, "save for a breech clout, as unhampered as September Morn," and bareback races by Umatilla Indian girls who shot "like iridescent streaks around the great oval." But officials of the roundup seemed proudest of stagecoach races in which the "old caravels of the plains" hurtled around the track behind four-horse teams with volunteer passengers clinging like barnacles to the off sides of the coaches to keep them from capsizing on the turns. And Pendleton boasted a ceremonial dance of Indians who would soon sink "forever below the horizon of time."

These early rodeos seemed like home to cowboys being subjected to the restrictions of civilization. Those gifted enough to hit the road as professional riders or ropers found themselves performing in cities — eventually even cities as outlandish as New York — but were able, while surrounded by their kind, to stamp into them as blithely as they had stamped into Cheyenne or Abilene when leading simpler lives.

The qualities that made the oldtime cowboy unique betrayed many of those who surrendered to more mundane existences after being forced off the range. They had a tendency to become butchers or bartenders in the wistful hope of preserving their independence, though their previous experiences with cattle or whiskey offered them little preparation for these new endeavors. But recklessness, improvidence, fortitude and clannishness sustained a man on the rodeo circuit as they had sustained him in the open spaces of Texas or Montana.

The rodeo cowboy lived a hand-to-mouth existence in the first decades of public riding, roping and bulldogging exhibitions. He found himself as often as not competing with local ranch hands for fancy saddles or other

Eloise Fox Hastings beams exultantly after throwing a steer.

When risks were not for men only

Rodeo has always been a tough and dangerous occupation that men might expect to dominate. But from its earliest days the ranks of contestants were infiltrated by women, who felt they had every right to compete for prizes and take their chances on broken bones. Rodeo was, in fact, one of the first sports in America in which women contended as professional athletes.

As early as 1904, women were being flipped over the heads of bucking horses and getting up to ride again. Within a decade, women's bronc riding had become a regularly scheduled, prize-paying event in several rodeos. The rules for men and women were basically the same, although women had the option — which some declined — of riding with stirrups tied together under the horse to help them stay in the saddle. Such slight dispensations indicated an "inherent chivalry" among cowboys and spectators, wrote an observer of a 1915-era rodeo, that "makes them shrink from witnessing injury to a woman."

Women soon became expert at other skills, like steer roping and bulldogging, and they graduated from long skirts to jodhpurs. But, as low prize money led to waning interest, women's participation in the more brutal, male-dominated rodeo events, such as bronc riding and steer wrestling, all but disappeared by the 1940s.

Bonnie McCarroll takes a nasty spill after her stirrup strap breaks at Pendleton in 1915. She died 14 years later, after a horse fell on her.

Lucille Mulhall signals triumphantly after roping and tying a steer at Cheyenne. She could rope as many as eight running horses at once.

equipment in lieu of actual cash. He compensated, when he could, for the meager rewards of the arena by touring with Wild West shows or, in later years, by working as a stunt man on the silent movie lots of Hollywood.

Show business lured a few cowboys from their accustomed haunts even before the day of rodeo. The most luckless, according to a widely repeated story, joined "The Daring Buffalo Chase of the Plains," which Wild Bill Hickok staged—or, rather, attempted to stage—at Niagara Falls, New York, in the spring of 1870. Dogs chased Hickok's buffalo through residential streets, his caged bear broke free and gobbled up sausages it commandeered from an alarmed Italian street vendor, and Wild Bill and his cowboys retreated to the freight yards and rode the rods back to Kansas. But Wild West shows offered cowboys long-term employment once Buffalo Bill and the Miller brothers of Oklahoma's vast 101 Ranch made the business a success.

Cowboys who caught on with Cody or the Millers might find themselves in Europe, or working with camels, elephants, female sharpshooters, Indians, Russian Cossacks, Mexican *vaqueros,* chorus girls, buffalo or even, in one instance, racing terrapins. For all that, they could polish their reputations while touring with Wild West shows—since they were performing for their professional peers in the cast as well as for startled spectators in the stands.

Few of the performers on the early rodeo/Wild West circuit specialized in a single event. Most of them paid entry fees in as many events as they could afford in the hope of finding luck—and cash—in at least one. Texan Leonard Stroud was a star bronc rider from 1914 to 1923, but he roped calves, bulldogged steers, entered relay races and competed as a fancy roper as well. He was the trick-riding champion of the rodeo world for 10 years, and became one of the first cowboys—thanks to his willingness to diversify—to eke out a living from prize money, but he still augmented his income by working with the Ringling Brothers Circus and the Pawnee Bill Show.

Some energetic cowboys, among them a bronc rider named Samuel (Booger Red) Privett, developed Western theatrical enterprises of their own. Privett, a Texan, had an instinct for making the best of adversity. A firecracker, which blew up in his face when he was 13, cost him an eye and left him badly disfigured. He bragged that he was the "world's ugliest man." He was orphaned at 15, became an itinerant horsebreaker, hunted work by defying the world to produce an outlaw he could not ride and, eventually, accumulated a string of bucking horses of his own.

He hit the road with them, drew small-town crowds by inviting all comers to try staying aboard them, and then lured ambitious local buckaroos into competing against him for money by offering to accept seemingly insuperable handicaps himself. Privett, his victims discovered, was fully capable of sticking to a bronc after mounting backward or while riding without using his hands. He saved his winnings, bought a tent and started his own small Wild West show. He became an institution in dusty corners of the Southwest and contributed, through his own brand of raw showmanship, to making the bronc rider an enduring symbol of the Old West.

But it took promoters, rather than cowboys like Stroud or small-time showmen like Privett, to make the rodeo a national institution: to develop its format, to sell its exciting amalgam of spectacle and sport and to amplify the echoes it struck from the American past. Not the least of these entrepreneurs were small-town businessmen who managed, through pride, energy and boosterism, to turn shows like those in Cheyenne and Pendleton into annual rites as reflective of the national psyche as the World Series or a Fourth of July parade.

But rodeo very probably owed more, in the long run, to enterprisers who risked their money on it out of the simple hope of hitting it rich. If any one man deserved credit for modernizing the rodeo it was Guy Weadick, a 101 Ranch roper-turned-promoter, who talked four wealthy Alberta cattlemen into backing him with $100,000 in 1912 to create the first Calgary Stampede. Weadick offered performers big money for the first time—a total of $20,000 in gold, with $1,000 guaranteed to each first-place winner in the major events—and thus altered the shape of the sport.

Cowboys ride in the grand march during a
Pendleton Round-Up sometime between
1910 and 1920. In 1914 one writer said
of the rodeo: "One feels the touch and
senses the romance of the passing West."

Weadick did not stop there. He offered another
$20,000 in prizes at Winnipeg the next year, and
raised the ante to $50,000 in promoting a New York
Stampede at Long Island's Sheepshead Bay in 1916.
This last big show all but broke him. It ran for 12 days,
but New York fell prey to a polio epidemic and a
subway strike, the large audiences he had expected did
not show up and he had to reduce the prize money he
had promised scores of cowboys and cowgirls who had
paid their way across the country to perform for dudes
in the East. His New York Stampede made rodeo
history, however. Those spectators who got to Long
Island were enthralled; Eastern newspapers gave it
banner headlines, and the publicity it generated created
audiences that rewarded other promoters later on.

The contestants, too, found the occasion a memorable experience. They were fascinated by New Yorkers

("like a bunch of ants," concluded one cowboy) and
did not leave without tincturing the color of life in the
big city, most dramatically while repelling a gang of
hoodlums who dressed up in cowboy hats and tried to
crash a party held for the visiting Westerners at Coney
Island. Some of the visitors were able, better yet, to
substantiate one treasured aspect of Western dogma:
that no Easterner knew beans about horses.

Weadick had shipped a hundred unbroken range
animals to New York for a wild-horse race, and auctioned them off after the rodeo, since they were not
worth the price of return transportation. Most of the
buyers were New York horse-cart peddlers who had
not the slightest experience with the sort of snorting
broomtails involved in the sale.

"Foghorn" Clancy, the Stampede's announcer,
wrote later: "There never was another show like that

one. I laughed until my sides ached when those fellows started to take their horses home. Here would go a horse with a huckster hanging on to the lead rope and being dragged across the lot at sixty miles an hour. Another horse would appear to be perfectly gentle and let himself be tied behind the buggy in which the man had come out. Then all at once the bronc would decide to join the wild bunch, kick out, turn the buggy over, break loose and be gone. There were wild horses and hucksters flying in every direction. Some of them never got their horses off the grounds. In a few minutes the place was such a bedlam of horses and men, all running madly in different directions with the men yelling and the horses whickering, that it was colossal. For a while it simply rained horses in Brooklyn."

Weadick's career as a free-lance promoter was cut short by his losses in 1916. He gave trick-roping exhibitions for several years and then settled down in Calgary to devote himself full time to its annual Stampede. But another high roller, John Van (Tex) Austin, stepped into the vacuum created by Weadick's surrender and demonstrated beyond all doubt that rodeo was becoming a national rather than a Western phenomenon. Audiences went wild during a 10-day,

20-performance rodeo that Austin produced at Madison Square Garden in 1922, and one New York newspaper reported:

" 'Tex' Austin has punctured a belief widely held that spectators for a rodeo had to be drawn from people more or less indigenous to the western cattle country. That is all bunk. New York is full of enthusiasts. At the Garden they stand in their seats and yell themselves hoarse. They behave like crazy folk." Austin capitalized on his successful debut at the Garden by bringing an even bigger rodeo to Yankee Stadium the following year, and he enjoyed six similar successes in Chicago between 1925 and 1930.

Pioneering rodeo promoters, like the cowboys who performed for them, were a versatile lot. Many were cowboys themselves. Rotund C. B. (Charlie) Irwin, one of the chief organizers of Cheyenne's Frontier Days, provided bucking horses, announced events, competed in them (setting a steer-roping record in 1906) and often hopped into the arena to hold plunging broncs as contestants struggled to mount. He owned a Wild West show, a string of race horses and a large ranch as well. And he found time to serve as a special agent for the Union Pacific Railroad, maintain-

1924. As rodeos grew in popularity, political organizations like the Klan sometimes turned out to push their causes among the crowds.

ing a specially rigged express car that could be loaded with Pinkerton men and fast horses at the first news of a train robbery. Irwin was a friend of many contestants and was described by cowboy humorist Will Rogers as the "best company that ever lived."

Not all promoters were so popular. The sport was flooded in the early part of the century with fast-buck artists who lured contestants to poorly financed rodeos with vague promises of large prizes, and then skipped town with the entry money and gate receipts. Cowboys accepted such losses philosophically during the early years, but began voicing their resentment in the 1930s. Much of their ire was focused on a man named Colonel William T. Johnson.

Johnson was not a fast-buck artist; he was one of the largest rodeo stock contractors and promoters of all time—and one of the most successful. His fast-paced rodeos, augmented with attractive cowgirls, were wildly popular with audiences, who turned out in record numbers for two- and three-week extravaganzas in New York and Boston in the late '20s and early '30s. But cowboys considered him a hard taskmaster.

They told themselves that he put them on the most dangerous broncs and Brahma bulls he could find as a means of avenging the death of his daughter—a girl who had married a cowboy and had been killed with him in an automobile accident while bound for a rodeo. And cowboys, who were proud of a tradition of generosity among themselves, were moved to a kind of repugnance by his meanness with money.

They were particularly outraged by a tale, widely circulated, concerning Johnson's treatment of one Herman Linder, who sold the promoter a bucking horse for $150 but was taken to a hospital, having been hurt during a rodeo ride, before being reimbursed. The management of Madison Square Garden donated some money to tide Linder over and Johnson, who volunteered to deliver this purse, was accused of telling Linder, on arriving at the cowboy's bedside, that he had come to pay for the horse.

Johnson was forced to pay for his parsimony in 1936. He pocketed contestant's entrance fees (instead of adding them to the prizes) during a rodeo he staged at Madison Square Garden and the cowboys refused to compete for him when he moved his show to Boston. He swore to run his stock into Boston harbor rather than accede to the strikers' demands, but he backed down in the end, staged the rodeo, and for the first time offered the kind of prize money the contestants felt they deserved for their hazardous performances. This Boston rodeo marked the end of Johnson's career as a promoter, but the beginning of a union of arena performers called The Cowboys Turtle Association ("We was slow as turtles in doing something like this"), which later became the Professional Rodeo Cowboys Association.

The names of few, if any, of these oldtime performers would be recognizable to the modern rodeo fan. Most of the buckaroos who thrilled audiences in the early years vanished without a trace when their riding days were done. Rodeo established a Hall of Fame in Oklahoma City in 1965, but visitors, though fascinated, tended to find its early "honorees" as unrecognizable as men memorialized on Civil War monuments.

Clay McGonagill, one of rodeo's earliest heroes, won more than 500 steer-roping events in the first decades of the 20th Century, and was such an artist that his successors were praised for "doing a McGonagill" when excelling with the lariat. Yet McGonagill's name means little to a rodeo fan today. This is also true of so famous a cowboy of the 1920s as Enos "Yakima" Canutt of Colfax, Washington—a man who would still be familiar to the public had he starred in some other sport. Canutt was tall, lean, handsome and so personable and talented that scores of Indians among the Palouse and Nez Percé tribes named their children for him. But few remember his feats in the arena; he is known chiefly for his long second career, after leaving the rodeo, as an actor and stunt man in Hollywood.

There is irony in the obscurity of early rodeo stars: the names of the most famous rodeo broncs of the era—chief among them Steamboat, Tipperary, Midnight and Five Minutes to Midnight—have survived as symbols of the Western legend long after the identities of most of the men who did battle with them have been forgotten. Canutt is credited, for instance, with being the first man ever to ride Tipperary, but Jon Cadwallader, an oldtimer who watched the job being done as a 13-year-old at Belle Fourche, South Dakota, remembered more about the horse—"a beautiful, breedy looking red chestnut gelding"—than about the man when asked to recall the historic moment. "That red horse," he said, could buck into "every known position. He'd leap sideways, he'd fall backwards, he'd

The black Westerners who missed the myth

One Wild West show impresario regarded him as "the greatest sweat and dirt cowhand that ever lived—bar none." He invented bulldogging, the forerunner of modern steer wrestling—the only standard rodeo event that can be traced to a single individual. Yet, like thousands of other black Westerners, Bill Pickett (opposite) is a dimly remembered figure, with none of the aura that surrounds the mythic heroes of the Old West.

On the great cattle drives, about one cowboy in six was black. Two of the 10 U.S. Cavalry regiments on the Indian frontier were all black. There were black scouts, sodbusters, prospectors and townsmen (as well as black cardsharps and cattle rustlers). But when the real Old West ended, the white mythmakers who were to carry its legend into the 20th Century simply left the blacks out.

Blacks were barely mentioned in the thousands of dime novels about the West; there were no black characters in Owen Wister's seminal, serious Western novel, *The Virginian*. And in Western movies, while Indians, Mexicans and Chinese were often maligned or misrepresented, blacks were hardly represented at all.

Bill Pickett's spectacular skills earned him a little more recognition than most of his black predecessors in the Old West. He could throw a steer without using his hands, forcing the beast to the ground with his teeth—sunk, bulldog-fashion, into the animal's lip. He was a star attraction on the rodeo and Wild West show circuit for more than 15 years after the turn of the century. But not until 1972, 40 years after his death, was he elected to the National Rodeo Cowboy Hall of Fame—the first black man who was so honored.

Bulldogger Bill Pickett, seen here at the height of his career, was billed for his rodeo appearances as "the Dusky Demon."

Three riders struggle to stay balanced atop their mounts during a Roman race in the 1920s. In this event each rider stood on the backs of two horses that were securely shackled together at their saddle straps.

jump straight into the air and twist until his belly looked straight up at the sky and all four legs would be flailing the air. Oh, he was fast!"

The most fabled of the early broncs was Steamboat, foaled at Chugwater, Wyoming, in 1896. He threw the vast majority of men who tried to ride him during a career that lasted nearly 15 years and was remembered for reasons above and beyond his jarring, straight-legged contortions. He not only appeared at the most prestigious rodeos, but he made himself unforgettable by whistling—through an old nose injury—like the Santa Fe Super Chief when bucking.

Steamboat was owned by promoter Charlie Irwin and for many years was one of the major attractions of the Cheyenne Frontier Days "World's Champion Bucking and Pitching Contest." Broncobusters from throughout the West came to Cheyenne half hoping, half fearing they would draw the horse known as "the King of the Plains." Most of the men who stuck to his back seem to have done so by methods that would not be allowed under latter-day rules: grabbing the saddle horn, holding the rein with both hands or refusing to spur. Legend has it that only two men, Thad Sowder of Cheyenne (1902) and Dick Stanley of Portland, Oregon (1908), managed to ride him properly when he was in good condition, and Stanley rode him on a muddy field that inhibited Steamboat's performance. But not by much, as is obvious from this report, which was printed in *The Denver Post* the following day:

"The minute they let go of old Steamboat's head, Stanley drove the spurs home. Up he went, straight into the air alighting with feet bunched, only to jump again, sideways this time. Every time he hit the ground Stanley gave him the steel and at last Steamboat zig-zagged across the field to the fence, jumping it, and took to the muddy track. As Steamboat whirled and went plunging up the homestretch, Stanley kicked his right foot out of the stirrup and raked the black horse fore and aft. This was the last straw and the horse which has unmade so many champions went wild. With his head between his knees he began to buck in circles, using every trick in an attempt to unseat the little man in the purple shirt. Stanley never left the saddle, and his right boot was never still for an instant. At last old Steamboat was getting enough, and the crowd, realizing that the black horse had at last found his master, broke into

a roar beside which all other cheering at this great show has been a whisper.

"'Stanley! Stanley! Stanley!' they yelled, and Stanley waved his arms around his head as Steamboat at last came to a standstill. The fight seemed over and Stanley, thoroughly worn out, relaxed. He had done something which no man had ever come near doing—spurred Old Steamboat and ridden him until he stopped bucking.

"But when Stanley relaxed, the cunning old devil thought he had found his chance. Down went his head once more, and with his back arched he made a terrific plunge into the air and sideways. It was an unexpected move, but it got him nothing. Stanley's boot drove him with a thud, and the steel reminded the champion bucking horse that the man from Portland was ready to continue the fight.

"A second time Stanley booted and spurred until Steamboat raised his head and came to a standstill, beaten this time beyond the shadow of a doubt. The

man grabbed the horse's head and Stanley slipped out of the saddle, reeled a few steps and fell into the arms of his friends.

"As he came down the track 15,000 people stood up to cheer him, and the yelling could have been heard for miles. He had beaten Old Steamboat to a finish and the crowd went mad with excitement and enthusiasm."

But neither Stanley nor any subsequent rider could break the horse's spirit. Steamboat bucked as furiously as ever until 1914, when he was destroyed as an act of mercy after developing blood poisoning from an accidental cut. Owner Charlie Irwin dispatched his game old campaigner with a rifle that had once belonged to the notorious Wyoming hired gun Tom Horn, and *The Wyoming Tribune* reported, in Steamboat's obituary that "the horse faced his executioners with his head up and a trace of his old fire in his eyes."

Steamboat was succeeded during the 1920s and 1930s by the "Two Midnights," a pair of coal-black bucking horses owned by a stock contractor named Verne Elliot and his partner, Ed McCarthy. Midnight, the older of the two, was dubbed "the devil horse" by cowboys who became convinced he could not be ridden. He proved most of them right during his 10-year prime as a peak performer. His reputation, by 1930, had become so formidable that contestants at Cheyenne asked that he be removed from the bucking finals—a petition that was denied by the rodeo committee on the ground that "this show bars neither man nor horse." But Midnight, for all his demonic behavior, was a pet in the stable and would let contractor Elliot's wife feed him lumps of sugar only minutes after humiliating yet another luckless cowboy in the arena.

Five Minutes to Midnight succeeded his stablemate as "the unrideable one," and was considered the best bucking horse in the country for 13 years. Both horses fared better than many a cowboy after making their last appearances. Verne Elliot retired his spectacular campaigners when cowboys began to stick to their backs, kept them in grass and oats through their declining

Daredevil tricks of the cowboy's trade

From the earliest days, impromptu acrobatics on horseback were a popular cowboy pastime, but it was not until 1893 that trick riding began to gain currency as a sport. In that year, Russian Cossacks appearing at the Chicago World's Columbian Exposition performed feats that the cattle drovers had never dreamed of. As reports of the dazzling show drifted west, cowboys began practicing the new tricks.

By 1910 the sport was standard rodeo fare. Trick riders were judged more on the speed of their horses and the variety of their stunts than on grace, and contests tended to be diverse and unpredictable. Nevertheless, some tricks became classics, like those shown here. A few, like Leonard Stroud's breathtaking layout *(below)*, were named for their famous inventors. Others varied from show to show, the performers practicing at night to keep the stunts secret until show time.

THE HIPPODROME STAND

THE STROUD LAYOUT

112

THE SIDE-STAND NECK STRADDLE

GOING UNDER THE BELLY

113

years and dug them adjoining graves (Midnight's in 1936, "Old Five's" in 1947) when they were finally claimed by death. He raised a tombstone over Midnight's last resting place that bore the inscription:

Under this sod lies a great bucking hoss;
There never lived a cowboy he couldn't toss.
His name was Midnight, his coat black as coal,
If there is a hoss-heaven, please God, rest his soul.

Rodeo's spectacular beasts were eventually upstaged by its cowboys; not only because one bronc or bull looks much the same as the next one to urban audiences (i.e. frightening) but because the sport began to attract millions of new followers who were fascinated with its star performers and the big risks and big money they pursued. This metamorphosis coincided, in the years after World War II, with the emergence of a reckless, handsome young broncobuster named Casey Tibbs, who lent rodeo a kind of glamor it had never possessed.

Tibbs — a rancher's son from Fort Pierre, South Dakota, who began breaking horses at age 10 — was not the only performer of the postwar era to dip into the big money or to win national recognition. Jim Shoulders of Henryetta, Oklahoma, (who rode both broncs and bulls) and Bill Linderman of Red Lodge, Montana, (who excelled in steer wrestling and saddle bronc riding) were fully as successful. The three of them took turns winning the All Around Cowboy Championship (rodeo's supreme honor based on total dollars earned in two or more events) during the 1950s and seldom earned less than $35,000 apiece during the years in which they dominated the sport. Larry Mahan, a personable, articulate bronc and bull rider from Brooks, Oregon, not only bested their records a bit later — winning the all-around championship six times — but made a name for himself as a speaker, teacher, author and TV personality as well.

But Tibbs, in his day, was the D'Artagnan, the Rhett Butler, the Bonnie Prince Charlie of the rodeo circuit. High school girls mooned over his pictures and older women were fascinated by his audacity, his easy smile and his air of boyish susceptibility — not to mention the glamor he achieved by appearing on the cover of LIFE magazine in 1951. But his dark, poetic good looks and air of fragility (he stood six feet tall but weighed only 150 pounds) masked exquisite reflexes

and an intuitive ability to commune with the plunging monsters that bore him — legs flailing, one arm high — into the arena when the chute was suddenly flung open.

Bronc riders, by the time Tibbs made his debut, were no longer required to ride an animal to a standstill as they were in Steamboat's day, but had simply — though the task was not simple at all — to stick to its back for 10 seconds as stylishly as fate would permit (the time was later reduced to eight seconds). Tibbs, who rode broncs both bareback and with a saddle, developed a rhythmic "rocking chair" style of riding that revolutionized the event. Many experts considered him the greatest bronc rider of all time.

He wore his aura of recklessness and indulged his hunger for sensation as tirelessly between rodeos as in the arena. He affected purple Cadillacs, drove them 95 miles an hour for endless thousands of miles a season, and edged them off the road on occasion to run over baggage belonging to some hapless hitchhiker — just for the hell of it. He took no offense, however, when some other cowboys lured him into running over a suitcase full of bricks they had thoughtfully planted along his route. And he engaged in barroom brawls with men bigger than himself just for the hell of it, too. "I don't have to last fifteen rounds like a boxer," he said. "I'm on and off a bronc before I can take a deep breath. But a rodeo cowboy's got a lot of determination and in a street fight he makes up for short wind that way."

He put up with injury and pain — his left ankle had been broken three times by the time he was 22, and he suffered many broken ribs — with the aid of whiskey. He carried a flask into the arena and took a few quick jolts before boarding a horse. But he drank to amplify life, too — often through sleepless days and nights of parties, of high-speed driving and of confrontation with the next horse before the next audience. Where, he was sometimes asked, did his money go? "I'm going to start saving," he would answer. "I'll have to start next year." He gambled with fervor, managing to lose $11,000 in one week of dice and poker in Nevada. "But if I died tomorrow I've had a hell of a life."

While Tibbs was making headlines and fascinating audiences with his own particular brand of magic, hundreds, then thousands of college and high school students were caught up in a rodeo craze that eventually — by providing professional rodeo with a kind of self-

Galloping past the grandstand, a trick roper encircles himself and his wife with "the big loop" at the Cheyenne Frontier Days Rodeo in 1945. Trick roping remained popular as a competitive rodeo event until the late 1920s, but thereafter it was performed usually as an exhibition.

A trick roper nimbly steps in and out of a small rope circle as he twirls a larger one over his head during the Trail Drivers Rodeo at San Antonio, Texas, in 1925.

energizing farm system—made more enduring contributions to the sport than he. This movement, which soon encompassed even grade-school kids, began with students in Western colleges who formed their own National Intercollegiate Rodeo Association in 1948. The college cowboys aped the professionals from the start: all contestants paid entrance fees, competed for cash, and drove day and night over weekends to escape the dread stigma of failing to make a ride.

College administrators did not know quite what to make of these mavericks of sport—many the sons and daughters of rodeo performers—in the beginning, but accepted them in the long run, eventually recruiting and subsidizing them for school-supported rodeo teams.

There was never a shortage of aspirants from which to choose. Cowboys bent on college were discovered, in many cases, to have begun their careers as children with the National Little Britches Rodeo Association, organized in 1961. Its sponsors introduced their charges to rodeo's trying events by organizing junior and senior divisions for both boys and girls and by arranging separate contests for each of these categories. Contestants of both sexes arrayed themselves in astonishing varieties of big hats, bright shirts, chaps, boots and spurs. Little cowpokes of eight or 10 begged, borrowed or stole cans of snuff and spat streams of brown fluid with a rakish air as they swaggered about, sizing one another up and doing their best to hide the fear and excitement that have always been part and parcel of rodeo at any level.

These dedicated buckaroos seemed to become even more obsessed with the attitudes and dress of the Old West when they reached high school. A thousand of them stood raptly at attention at Helena, Montana, during one of the national rodeos held for them in the 1970s while an announcer intoned something entitled The Rodeo Prayer: "Help us, Lord, to live our life in such a manner that when we make the last inevitable ride to the country up there where the grass grows lush green and stirrup high and the water runs cool, clear and deep, that You as our last judge will tell us that our entry fees are paid."

The romantic sentiments of this creed masked the realistic attitudes of those for whom it was composed. Many junior competitors, conditioned from childhood to regard the working skills of the frontier as competitive athletic events, thought of rodeo in terms of hard cash. High-school performers were allowed to compete against professionals in some states without losing their standing as amateurs and a gifted few were able to collect sizable purses, as well as the more traditional rewards of silver belt buckles and fancy saddles.

These young cowboys fitted easily into a world that would have left drifters from the old open ranges dumfounded. By the 1950s rodeo had acquired the inevitable trappings of any big-time professional sport: press agents, beauty queens, entertainers, souvenir peddlers and millions of enthusiastic fans. It offered fortunes in prize money. It inspired dozens of self-appointed teachers who set up schools for ropers and riders, schools for managers, schools for announcers, schools for promoters, schools for rodeo clowns, even schools to teach aspiring rodeo queens how to apply make-up and sit gracefully upon a horse.

The schools themselves relied on educational methods that would have further astounded denizens of the Old West. They taught modish psychological stratagems designed to put contestants in a winning frame of mind and used mechanical marvels that promised quick results by short-circuiting the dusty arena apprenticeships that had once forged rodeo champions.

A Texas construction boss named Sam Reeves began devoting his spare time in the late 1960s to the creation of a machine capable of duplicating the motions of a bucking horse or a Brahma bull. He labored for more than a year to perfect a device he called the Gold Nugget Rider Trainer, a wall-eyed, one-legged fiberglass beast that unseated aspiring bronc tamers as peremptorily as old Steamboat himself once did.

Reeves was not the first to experiment in this peculiar field of dynamics. No rodeo stock contractor in his right mind ever let cowboys practice on his valuable animals and early bronc riders schooled themselves on homemade "bucking barrels"—casks hung from rafters or tree limbs by ropes and springs and yanked about by whooping colleagues or perspiring relatives. Former champ Jim Shoulders improved on this rude concept in the mid-1960s by connecting an oil drum to the universal joint of a partially dismantled automobile and activating it by throwing the car's gearshift lever from forward to reverse and back again. And while Reeves worked to create something worthier of 20th Cen-

Casey Tibbs's appearance on the cover of LIFE *(above)* made him a glamorous figure, but he still had to take his chances in the arena like any other rodeo cowboy. At right he sits uneasily on a bronc named War Paint just before a ride in 1958. Although Tibbs had successfully ridden the horse before, War Paint took only three seconds to throw him this time, causing Tibbs to remark: "I wonder if he's getting smarter or I'm getting dumber."

Rodeo clowns taunt an enraged Brahma bull, enticing the animal to spend its fury against a sturdy barrel instead of goring a hapless cowboy it has thrown into the dust, just out of range of this photograph.

tury technology, another inventor, Joe D. Turner of Albuquerque, New Mexico, produced an electrically powered bucking machine he called Bronco-El Toro.

These bucking machines brought a new dimension to the development of bronc and bull riders. Turner sold hundreds of his devices to colleges and high schools, and Reeves used his rider-trainers to lure students—among them, top professional contestants—to training courses he offered in Fort Worth. He augmented his hydraulically operated broncs with a weight room, whirlpool baths and gym equipment and subjected his students to lectures on goal setting, self-image and the subconscious mind.

Among the other enterprisers who began to cash in on rodeo's burgeoning popularity in the 1950s were the cowboys themselves. Those with reputations to exploit set up their own schools, endorsed Western clothing, marketed lines of rodeo equipment and tried their hands at show business. Casey Tibbs failed to become a star on going to Hollywood after leaving rodeo, but his reputation landed him jobs as a movie bit player and stunt man. He promoted rodeo tours and clothing as well, and went into real estate, selling California lots he called "ranchettes." Wyoming's Chris LeDoux, a champion bareback rider, achieved peripheral fame as a composer and singer of Western ballads. He recorded songs with titles like "Tight Levi's and Yellow Ribbons" and "Them Bareback Horses," and hurried off to Nashville for recording sessions whenever his schedule permitted.

But none of this diluted the rigors of the arena itself, nor alleviated the danger, tension and exhaustion that had always been the lot of the cowboy. Chris LeDoux put up with pain as often and as stoically, for all his excursions into music, as any 19th Century bronco-buster. He broke a knee when a pickup horse collided with his wildly gyrating mount on one occasion, but began competing again six months later and suffered an equally aggravating injury as a reward. "Pulled my riggin' too tight. I was on Molly Brown and I could feel my collar bone pull in two while I was riding." He got on a horse named Smokey a month later and suffered a second separation during the ride. He responded by asking an athletic trainer to show him how to tape the shoulder—"It's that tape that holds me together . . . I'd fall apart without it"—and won $4,912,

119

4 | The cowboy President

"It was still the Wild West in those days, the far West, the West of Owen Wister's stories and Frederic Remington's drawings, the West of the Indian and the buffalo-hunter, the soldier and the cow-puncher."

What Theodore Roosevelt omitted from his 1913 autobiography was that the late-19th Century West was also *his* West—a West whose vigor and exaggerated masculinity, wrote a friend, "entered into the very marrow of his being" during the years he spent as a Dakota rancher in the 1880s. Through books about his own Western adventures and a popular history he wrote called *The Winning of the West,* he forcefully impressed his personal vision of the frontier on the American consciousness.

Moreover, as President, Roosevelt gave the Western experience greater prominence and wider application in the life of the United States than any writer or artist ever could, justifying imperialism abroad and trust-busting at home by citing the frontier traditions of expansionism and zealous safeguarding of the rights of the individual. He made the West of fact and legend the birthright of the entire nation, a heritage that even urban Easterners could claim as their own.

"I owe more than I can ever express to the West," Roosevelt wrote. "In that land we felt the beat of a hardy life in our veins and ours was the glory of work and the joy of living." He made it his life's purpose to infuse all of America with the Western spirit.

Theodore Roosevelt *(right)* pauses on a Colorado trail while hunting bear. The 1905 outing was Roosevelt's last big-game hunt as President and he did himself proud, bagging three "good big ones."

An irrepressible frontier spirit

Theodore Roosevelt was unable to resist lime-light: he wanted, said his daughter Alice, "to be the corpse at every funeral, the bride at every wedding and the baby at every christening." And there was an unquenchable boyishness about him. "You must always remember," his longtime English friend Cecil Arthur Spring-Rice once wrote in explaining the irrepressible Rooseveltian enthusiasm, "that the President is about six."

Both of these traits were involved in the fervor with which Teddy embraced the West after he decided to forsake New York for life as a cattleman in Dakota Territory. He rode 20 miles across the Badlands, practically as soon as he got off the train in 1884, to order a buckskin shirt from a Mrs. Maddox of Sand Creek. He took an inordinate amount of pride in this garment, which he considered to be "the most picturesque and distinctively national dress ever worn in America," and he took it to New York on a trip back East to have himself photographed in it, rifle in hand, "facing dangerous game," as an intimate commented with glee, "which was not there."

Not that he shirked dangerous game: he was mad about hunting despite his eyesight, which, even when corrected by the spectacles that were to become a political trademark, was never of the best. "Cocking my rifle and stepping quickly forward," he wrote his sister, Anna, during one hunting trip, "I found myself face to face with the great bear, who was less than 25 feet off. Doubtless my face was pretty white." But his rifle barrel was "steady as a rock" and the "great brute"

A penny shot into the tree trunk of this cast-iron Teddy Roosevelt bank causes the bear's head to pop up. In the real-life 1902 incident that inspired the toy, Teddy refused to shoot a helpless cub.

of a grizzly was soon in its "death agony"—as were deer, elk, antelope and lesser bears in the months that followed. But the embryo rancher pined for something rarer and scribbled a note in 1886 to Jack Willis, a commercial hunter at Thompson Falls, Montana:

"I want to shoot a white antelope goat. I have heard it is the hardest animal in the Rockies to find and the most difficult to kill. I have also heard that you are a great hunter. If I come to Montana will you act as my guide, and do you think I can kill a white goat?"

Willis had a terrible time trying to decipher this message—Roosevelt's handwriting was execrable—and suspected that its author might be a practical joker of some sort. He replied: "If you can't shoot any better than you can write, NO."

Roosevelt disregarded this discouraging response, sent the hunter a telegram asking him to be ready for action in five days, and took a train to Montana with his ranch foreman, William Merrifield. Roosevelt, then 27 years old, was a lithe and muscular young man, having devoted himself to rigorous exercise during boyhood and to boxing, as a lightweight, during four years at Harvard. He had served two terms as a legislator in the New York State Assembly, had rubbed shoulders with ward bosses and lobbyists, and had gained in the rough-and-tumble of practical politics a kind of self possession not necessarily bestowed by education and inherited wealth. But Willis bridled at the very sight of him. Roosevelt, said the backwoodsman, "had on corduroy knickers and a coat of a tenderfoot. He had red cheeks like a brewer's son and looked too much like a dude to make any hit with me."

"I'm here," the dude shouted. "When do we start?"

"*We* are not going to start," said Willis. "You can start whenever you like, so far as I'm concerned."

"Why not?" cried Roosevelt. "I'll pay you $25 for every shot you get me at a white goat!"

"I won't work for anyone on salary," responded Willis. "I go where I like and when I like and do as I darn well please."

Roosevelt dug into his baggage and hauled out an antique Sharps rifle. "I've brought you a present. It was hard to get, too. I had to hunt two days before I found that gun."

"That was because it's old-fashioned," said the hunter. "I'll be just as good a fellow as you are. I'll give it right back to you."

But Willis relented in the end—won over, despite himself, by Roosevelt's enthusiasm and frankness. He was about to head into the mountains on a hunting trip and agreed to let the newcomers tag along, but he warned them that they would have to subsist on bacon, beans, dried apples and black tea, and would have to look after themselves. "I won't act as a wet nurse for any man. I'll get you plenty of shots at goats. What you do with them is none of my business and you won't pay me for them."

"Bully," cried Roosevelt. "Now let's hurry."

Willis found himself torn between bemusement, exasperation and astonishment from that moment onward—while simultaneously admiring his new companion's unfailing cheerfulness in the face of hardship and mischance.

The hunter caught Roosevelt at an odd exercise in subterfuge after the three men had entered the main range of the Rockies on a stream named Vermilion Creek, unloaded their pack horses and set up a base camp. Pheasants were plentiful and Willis bagged a few for the pot—by shooting off their heads with a rifle. Roosevelt set out to emulate him, but discovered that he was incapable of this trick of marksmanship; he was apparently unable to quite tolerate the fact (as in later life he would find himself unable, when recalling that he had been lightweight champion of Harvard, to quite remember not having been lightweight champion at all). Willis came upon him trying to compensate by putting one foot on a downed bird's head and yanking hard as he picked it up.

The future President grinned gamely at the ridicule this earned him, but was subject to more serious dilemmas in the following days—one inadvertent, one self-imposed—that made Willis wonder whether he was lacking in ordinary common sense. Neither Roosevelt nor his foreman had bothered to equip himself with hobnailed shoes. Merrifield set out in high-heeled cowboy boots, which forced him to walk downhill backward to keep his balance and blistered his feet so badly that he eventually refused to stir from camp. Roosevelt insisted on wearing heel-less, slippery, moccasin-like shoes he had used in the Maine woods, but he did much better than Merrifield—half trotting to keep pace with the long-striding Willis and pausing only to wipe steam from his glasses—until a day when he and the hunter found themselves edging along a high, narrow, cliffside ledge.

Roosevelt's shoes slipped and Willis, turning, saw him "disappearing, head foremost, over that sharp edge with his rifle still in his hand. I wouldn't have given two bits for his life for it was easily a sixty-foot fall and the bottom was covered with jagged rocks. But he struck first in the top of a tall pine tree, bounded into the outstretched arms of a second tree, and then into the branches of a third one, finally landing on a bunch of moss that was thick as a feather bed." The startled Willis, peering into the depths from his risky position, heard his vanished charge yelling, "Not hurt a bit. Wait till I find my glasses."

Roosevelt had a way of growing on Westerners, in part because he struck them as such a curious creature, and in part because he assumed that he had assimilated their skills and attitudes by the simple act of settling among them and was eager to match them in endurance and courage to prove it. Willis, a philosopher of sorts, decided that his guest had escaped because "God loves a brave man." He was impressed, moreover, by the unrelenting vigor with which Roosevelt scrambled over the harsh terrain—mile after mile for two long days—to track and finally kill a goat that he had wounded when granted his first shot of the expedition. Some of the successful nimrod's excitement at this triumph rubbed off on the Montanan, for he agreed to a wearing chore: making the 12-mile round trip back to camp in order to fetch the complaining ranch foreman and a big, glass-negative camera that Roosevelt had insisted on bringing into the mountains, so Merrifield could take a picture of the two of them beside the defunct animal.

Willis soon encountered a more disconcerting consequence of his guest's enthusiasms. Roosevelt discov-

ered a waterfall that plunged 300 feet into a steep gorge, and insisted that Willis and Merrifield tie two 100-foot ropes together and lower him down the cliff with his bulky camera, thereby enabling him to do pictorial justice to the scene. Willis protested, but eventually gave in—snubbing the line around a tree as he and Merrified paid it out—and was rewarded as the photographer, at this point dangling 60 feet above the turbulent pool below the falls, shouted up with satisfaction that he had achieved just the proper perspective. However, the scheme's flaw was shortly evident: Willis and Merrifield could not pull him back up again. Roosevelt shouted for them to cut the rope, explaining that he was a good swimmer.

Willis had the good sense to veto this airy suggestion. He hurried back to their camp, found 50 feet of lighter rope, doubled it, added it to the line and managed to lower its victim a little closer to the pool. Willis then worked his way down the gorge, cut logs, bound them into a crude raft with vines and pushed it along the shore until he was able to catch the camera when Roosevelt tossed it. Merrifield then cut the rope and Willis hauled the photographer to safety aboard the shaky float. This took some doing. Roosevelt had been hanging in the loop of the rope—without complaint—for two hours and his arms and chest were bruised and numb; he "came down like a stone" into the icy pool, was stunned by the impact

These spurs, worn by Roosevelt in the 1880s, have silver conchas, or disks, inlaid in gold with the Maltese-cross brand of his first ranch *(top)* and the symbol of his second, the Elkhorn *(bottom)*.

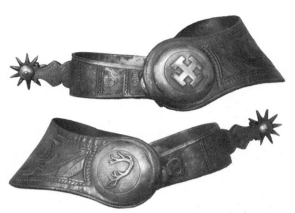

and was only half-conscious when the hunter pulled him out of the water.

These adventures in Montana as well as similar escapades that tested Roosevelt against the rigors of life in Dakota Territory had a profound effect upon his philosophy, although his career as a practicing rancher lasted little more than two years. He had been driven west by the sense of loss he felt at the deaths of both his first wife and his mother. He married again in 1886—taking to wife a childhood friend, Edith Carow—and returned to the East after his cattle (and with them his $52,500 investment in Western life) were largely wiped out by blizzards in the awful winter of 1886-1887. However, he remained a Westerner at heart and later said that the days he spent in the West were "the most important educational asset of all my life." Ranching, he said, "taught a man self-reliance, hardihood, and the value of instant decision."

He went so far as to say that had he not gone west as a young man, he might never have become President of the United States. His analysis of the chain of events connecting these two phases of his life was plausible: his experience with Westerners had convinced him "that the men were just the kind to have with me if ever it became necessary to go to war"; he acted on this belief by raising a regiment of frontiersmen, the Rough Riders, when the Spanish-American War began; and the fame he won as their leader swept him into the New York governor's mansion and, eventually, the White House.

But the West's effect on the life of Teddy Roosevelt was no more profound than the effect he had upon the West—both on the idea of the Old West that survived the passing of the frontier to suffuse the whole nature of modern America and on the 20th Century reality of the land itself. His dauntless and unrelenting enthusiasm and his towering stature as a writer and national leader enabled him to imbue the nation with his own concept of the West and to give that concept the power of public policy in matters ranging from

conservation to international relations. To some substantial degree both the West that we remember and the West that we have were the creations of Theodore Roosevelt.

His works as a popular writer were widely read and did a great deal to change the Easterner's notion of the Old West as a place of casual savagery and smoking pistols to that of a society that, while it was harsh and demanding, seriously aspired to lofty ideals. "No man can really understand our country, and appreciate what it really is and what it promises," he wrote, "unless he has the fullest and closest sympathy with the ideals and aspirations of the West." Roosevelt wholeheartedly embraced those ideals as he understood them—an egalitarianism that enabled every strong, virtuous and hardworking person to make his own way; the right of an individual to defend his own just interests with force; and, above all else, the expansion of civilization, particularly American civilization, into "barbarian" territory.

He carried these precepts into his Presidency, stamping national policy with the ethos of the Old West, as he interpreted it. A nation, like an individual, according to Roosevelt, has to act with "vigorous manliness." He thought that the world was analogous to the savage prairie and believed that the United States was duty bound to draw quickly against shifty, venal or decadent enemies. American imperialism, which flourished throughout his administration, was as right and logical, he contended, as was the taking of the West from its original inhabitants, the Indians—and as to the rightness and logic of that conquest he had no doubts whatsoever.

The same spirit motivated his reforms in the country's domestic affairs. Individuals, not giant corporations or political machines, had won the West, and in the process had evolved their own democratically elected governments and laws to protect them against wrongdoers. Self-help was the first rule of the frontier, he said, but cooperation was the second. The 20th Century American deserved the same kind of protec-

"You would be amused to see me," wrote 25-year-old Teddy to a friend before this picture was taken, "in my fringed and beaded buckskin shirt, horsehide *chapara-jos* or riding trousers, and cowboy boots."

Roosevelt and comrades Wilmot Dow (*left*) and William Sewall (*right*) make a haggard trio after capturing three boat thieves in 1886.

tion against greedy monopolies and political bosses that frontier communities had given the individual settler against rampaging outlaws.

Roosevelt's admiration for the West went beyond its hardy people and the virtues of its institutions. He was in love with the land itself, and in no cause did he work with more devotion or effect as a national leader than that of conserving the natural beauty and natural wealth of the region for Americans of the future. Whether they know it or not, those who enjoy today the grand scenery and the wild game of the West, as well as those who benefit from its lumber-producing forests, and the reservoirs and water-distribution systems that make possible its agricultural abundance, are indebted to hunter Willis for rescuing his dude companion from the icy Montana pool.

Roosevelt was a complex being, as all of this would suggest, and the assumption held by many—that he was simply a bounding extrovert with gold-rimmed glasses, a lot of teeth, a one-word vocabulary ("Bully!") and a passion for blasting large animals both at

home and abroad—discredits the whole man. His writing about the West tended toward the epic in tone, and he had no hesitations about injecting himself and his views into his work, but he nevertheless produced some of the most considered and original prose about prairie life, Western hunting and Western history ever written in the United States. He envied his friend Owen Wister's facility with words but was himself immensely readable.

He did not lack an instinct for scholarship, even though he was guided in practicing it, on occasion, by his own excited view of the world. He was a bibliophile, an early speed reader (in English—he had to go a little slower in French, German and Italian, and labored over Latin and Greek) who tore through books at an astonishing pace, was addicted to the printed word, and, with the exception of Thomas Jefferson, was probably the most knowledgeable person in literature, science and philosophy ever to serve in the White House.

He read everywhere. Aides found him submerged in Herodotus (he could only be aroused, when reading, by a blow on the back) while thousands bawled, "We want Teddy!" at the 1912 Republican Convention. Lawrence Abbott, a friend who sought him when he was late for dinner on a train running between Khartoum and Cairo in 1910, discovered him "in one of the white enamelled lavatories, standing under an electric light, oblivious to time and surroundings" and deep in Lecky's *History of Rationalism in Europe*. He had a taste for the classics—Tacitus and Polybius (but not Livy) as well as Homer, the Bible and Dante—but could dive into a *History of the James Brothers* or *Mrs. Wiggs of the Cabbage Patch* with fervor.

Roosevelt studied hard at Harvard in a period when study was unfashionable among undergraduates, and drafted the opening chapters of his first book, *The Naval War of 1812*, while still at Cambridge. He emerged into the world of affairs with an inherited income of about $8,000 a year—his father having left the family a fortune of $750,000—but set out to supplement it by writing because he wanted "butter and jam" even though "I had enough to get bread." He gave himself an edge most writers lacked by buying a partnership in the publishing house of G. P. Putnam's Sons for $20,000 (though he was so careless with money that he did not bother to discover that he had but $10,000 in the bank and had to ask an uncle, James Roosevelt, to bail him out when his check bounced).

He turned to his pen in dead earnest, while in the Dakota Badlands in 1885, to express his growing fascination with the horizons, the animals, the men and the history of the American West. He described personal hardship and personal adventure in three books—*Hunting Trips of a Ranchman, Ranch Life and the Hunting Trail* and *The Wilderness Hunter*—which he produced in the next eight years. He told his readers, with particular satisfaction, about capturing three thieves who stole a boat he used as a kind of ferry at a point where his ranch was bisected by the Little Missouri River.

"In any wild country," he wrote, "where the power of the law is little felt or heeded, and where everyone has to rely upon himself for protection, men soon get to feel that it is in the highest degree unwise to submit to any wrong without making an immediate and resolute effort to avenge it upon the wrongdoers." He ordered his ranch hands to build a rude scow to be used in pursuit, appointed two of them as his personal posse, and stayed up late rehearsing lines he expected to speak on coming face to face with the quarry: a "hard case" named Mike Finnigan "who had been the chief actor in a number of shooting scrapes" and a pair of drifters who had attached themselves to him. A ranch guest, Fredrick Badger of Boston, said he was awakened to hear his host tramping up and down behind a curtain that separated their beds, repeating over and over, "I've got the gun on you. I know you stole my boat and I'm here to claim it."

Finnigan, as things turned out, needed little convincing. He and his toughest ally, a half-Indian named Burnsted, were off hunting when the avengers came upon the stolen boat and grabbed a "weak and shiftless" fellow named Pfaffenbach who had been left on guard. The missing thieves surrendered when ambushed upon their return, although Finnigan "hesitated, his eyes fairly wolfish, before realizing that he had no show, and, with an oath, let his rifle drop." The miscreants submitted, with equal docility, to the lens of their captor's ever-present camera, posing sheepishly while Roosevelt pointed his rifle at them. But they had to be watched, day and night, for the following 10 days, the first six of which were spent drifting farther downstream through ice jams. Roosevelt, who went without sleep for the last 36 hours as he herded the thieves across wintry country, was a tired, hungry and bedraggled figure when he finally turned them over to a sheriff.

These books of personal reminiscence had weaknesses. Roosevelt tended to repeat himself, and to engage too heavily in superlative. But their virtues far outweighed their failings for readers—and also for critics, to whom, as one put it, his "vivid pictures of windswept prairie and baldface mountain, of lovely, sweet-smelling flowers and endless virgin forests" were fresh, new and unexpected.

The West moved Roosevelt, at times, to a style close to poetry. Rising before dawn, he heard "a skylark singing, soaring up above me so high that I could not make out his form in the gray morning light . . . the music never ceased for a moment, coming down clear, sweet and tender from the air above." And he felt the "iron desolation" of the plains in winter when winds roar "in a thunderous bass as they sweep across the prairie or whirl through naked canyons" or when, with such gales stilled, a "merciless, terrible cold broods over the earth like the shadow of silent death. In the long nights there is no sound to break the lifeless silence. Lighted only by the wintry brilliance of the stars, the snow clad plains stretch out into endless wastes of glimmering white."

But these books, while they sprang directly from his infatuation with the wild, were only prelude to the work that was dearest to his heart and that must be considered his highest literary accomplishment: *The Winning of the West,* a historical appraisal of Americans who pushed through the Appalachians into the vast land beyond, and of the hostile Indians and hostile Europeans they encountered in doing so.

He completed but four of six volumes he planned when he sat down to write in 1888—*The Winning of the West* ends with the Louisiana Territory newly purchased from the French and with Lewis and Clark newly returned from the West Coast—but he inferred a great deal about "the army of fighting settlers, who, with axe and rifle, won their way from the Alleghenies to the Rio Grande and the Pacific." And he reflected, above all, that sense of grandeur, of saga, that has been echoed in so much of Western legend since. Roosevelt believed that the American frontiersman personified three centuries of ascendancy by English-speaking peoples and that his seizure of the continent was "the great, epic feat in the history of our race."

He hoped, in celebrating this accomplishment, to produce something that "would really take rank as in the very first class" and scoured libraries, private collections, and the faded diaries and letters of forgotten pioneers in his passion for authenticity and revealing detail. He utilized a good deal of this research, moreover, with a shrewd and judicious eye. *The Winning of the West* is full of splendidly bellicose footnotes in which he takes backwoods braggarts, self-serving soldiers and slovenly writers to task—casting a jaundiced eye, for instance, on George Rogers Clark's account of the capture of Vincennes, and giving the back of his hand to "small Western historians" for "absurd inflation of their language."

He deprived himself of the top literary ranking for which he thirsted by his fervor for warlike deeds and his

imperialist's view—attitudes that caused critics to accuse him of a lack of reflection, an excess of partisanship, something called "presentism" (which roughly meant viewing past events in modern terms rather than in their historical context) and an inability to "consistently hold the high ground." But *The Winning of the West* is an impressive work for all that, and remains a fascinating, informative and wonderfully readable piece of Americana. It filled a vacuum in its day. Roosevelt must be placed near Frederick Jackson Turner, the historian who conceived the frontier thesis, for having drawn his countrymen's attention to the West's influence on national goals and national character, and for doing so in a period when much of public assumption about the vanishing frontier stemmed from potboilers and haphazard accounts in newspapers.

Turner, in fact, became his instant admirer. "Mr. Roosevelt has done a real service to our history," he wrote in reviewing the final volume, "and has rescued a whole movement in American development from the hands of unskillful annalists." Roosevelt's work, according to Turner, "will be to the general reader a revelation." The two men looked at western expansion from vastly different points of view. Roosevelt, as he told Turner, was "more interested in the men themselves than in the institutions through and under which they worked." However, he, too, had a sense of the catalytic effect of the Western experience that Turner celebrated in his work. The frontier had created a race of men, Roosevelt wrote, "who differed from the rest of the world—even the world of America, and infinitely more, the world of Europe—in dress, in customs and in mode of life."

He devoted a great deal of research, thought and space to Indians, who had combined themselves with the rigors of the wilderness to oppose and thus to forge this new breed of "peculiar and characteristically American people." He provided insights into Indian culture about which most of his readers were ignorant, and wrote with admiration of these forest dwellers' prowess as hunters, agriculturists, trackers and warriors. But Indians were villains in *The Winning of the West.* Roosevelt was moved to indignation, it is true, by whites who massacred or brutalized Indians after promising them safety or peace, but he had little patience with "sentimental historians" who "speak as if

all the blame had been all ours and the wrong all done to our foes."

"Not only were the Indians very terrible in battle," he wrote, "but they were cruel beyond all belief in victory; and the gloomy annals of border warfare are stained with their darkest hues because it was a war in which helpless women and children suffered the same hideous fate that so often befell their husbands and fathers. The hideous unnameable, unthinkable tortures practiced by the red men on their captured foes were such as we read of in no other struggle." (He put his opinion more bluntly during a lecture in 1886: "I don't go so far as to think that the only good Indians are dead Indians, but I believe nine out of every ten are, and I shouldn't like to inquire too closely into the case of the tenth.") War with the tribes had been inevitable "unless we were willing that the whole continent West of the Alleghenies should remain an unpeopled waste. Had we refrained from encroaching on the Indi-

an lands, the Indians would have encroached on ours."

The Winning of the West performed a legitimate and stirring function: leading the reader ever west with the backwoodsman—into his forest clearings for weddings, dances, house raisings and defenses of isolated blockhouses; into the battles he fought at Great Kanawha, Kings Mountain and Fallen Timbers; and into an understanding of those rude political concepts by which he produced such experimental little governments as those of the Watauga Commonwealth and of the "lost state" of Franklin in Tennessee.

"The warlike borderers who thronged across the Alleghenies, the restless and reckless hunters, the hard, dogged frontier farmers, by dint of grim tenacity overcame and displaced Indians, French and Spaniards alike. They were led by no one commander; they acted under orders from neither king nor congress; they were not carrying out the plans of any far sighted leader. In obedience to the instincts working half blindly within

Roosevelt's Sagamore Hill home reflects the predilections of its occupant: bison from an 1883 Dakota hunt flank two Western bronzes *(right)*, while his Rough Rider hat hangs from Wyoming elk antlers *(left)*. The elephant tusks *(foreground)* were a gift from the Emperor of Ethiopia.

their breasts, spurred ever onward by the fierce desires of their eager hearts, they made in the wilderness homes for their children, and by so doing wrought out the destinies of a continental nation."

It was, Roosevelt noted repeatedly, the "warlike skill" and "adventurous personal prowess" of the settlers that pushed the frontier westward. "A race of peaceful, unwarlike farmers would have been helpless before such foes as the red Indians." The backwoodsmen "suffered terrible injuries at the hands of the red men," but "they waged a terrible warfare in return. They were of all men the best fitted to conquer the wilderness and hold it against all comers." And he believed that such men, himself not least among them, were still best-fitted to win and hold America's rightful place in the world—a view that was to advance his career in politics even if it hampered his progress in the arena of letters.

Roosevelt had hurried back to politics as he retreated from cattle ranching. He supported Benjamin Harrison's successful campaign for the Presidency, got himself appointed to the U.S. Civil Service Commission as a consequence, and spent six years learning to make his way in official Washington. He toiled over *The Winning of the West* in his spare time until 1896, but abandoned it after getting its fourth volume into print and after moving back to New York for engrossing service as one of the big city's four police commissioners. He did not return to the history, though he continued to hope for years that he would complete it. But politics was leading him toward a gaudier role in Western legend than he could ever have gained by writing: the colonelcy of the fabled Rough Riders and celebration of that fact on the front pages of every newspaper in the land.

He was an unusually uncompromising politician. President Harrison was dismayed at the zeal with which he fought the spoils system in Washington, and the New York cops were flabbergasted by the energy with which he railed against corruption, roved the streets at night to spy on dozing patrolmen, and shut up saloons on Sunday—alienating voters, in this last matter, who held beer more sacred than the law. Bigwigs of the Republican Party grew wary of giving him opportunity for further disturbances, and some actively opposed him, although it was politically risky to pub-

In 1899 players of this game—moving the markers to spins of the center disk—tracked Roosevelt's career to the Albany, New York, governor's mansion. In 1901, former Assistant Navy Secretary Roosevelt was in Washington as Vice President; that city became the game's goal.

licly snub one so adept at cultivating reporters and generating favorable publicity and who was so widely heralded as the most honest and fearless of the party's young men.

President William McKinley was no exception. Roosevelt had campaigned for him without stint but McKinley could not repress anxiety when Senator Henry Cabot Lodge called on him to report that his friend TR, as Roosevelt became known, wanted to be Assistant Secretary of the Navy. "I hope," said Mc-

Kinley, "he has no preconceived notion which he would wish to drive through the moment he got in." He was soon to discover—Lodge having talked him around by telling him not to anticipate "the slightest uneasiness on that score"—that he had been asking a wildcat to stick to a diet of barley soup.

Roosevelt itched for wars by which "the honor of the American flag" could be upheld, "stock-jobbing timidity" discouraged, and "futile sentimentalists of the international arbitration type" put in their places or, better yet, in jail. He had asked the War Department to allow him to organize "as utterly reckless a set of desperadoes as ever sat in a saddle" to invade Mexico in 1886, when there was trouble on the border. He hoped for "a bit of a spar" with Germany in 1889 when the United States turned briefly critical of the Kaiser, and told his English friend Cecil Arthur Spring-Rice that "the burning of New York" would be a "good object lesson" for those who opposed improved coast defenses. He advocated "a muss" with England a few years afterward when the British appeared to be bent on adding some Venezuelan territory to their colony in Guiana. "He regards one foe as good as another," cried Philosopher William James, "and swamps everything together in one flood of abstract bellicose emotion."

McKinley (who had "no more backbone," Roosevelt thought, "than a chocolate eclair") restrained him early in 1898 when he wanted to support rebellion against Spain in Cuba by sending a "flying squadron" to shoot up Barcelona and Cadiz. And McKinley went right on hoping to avoid hostilities with Spain after the battleship *Maine,* sent to Havana to mute warmongers in the United States, blew up there on February 15. It took Roosevelt but 10 days to demonstrate the "virile, manly qualities" he felt the country in danger of losing. On the afternoon of February 25 Navy Secretary John D. Long left him in charge of the department (after warning him against "taking steps affecting policy"), and Roosevelt wasted not a moment in ordering Admiral George Dewey, then commanding the U.S. Asiatic Squadron, to assemble his ships at Hong Kong and to prepare for "offensive operations in the Philippine Islands," which at the time were a Spanish possession.

War came and Dewey, thanks to Roosevelt, was able to defeat a Spanish fleet in Manila Bay just five days after hostilities began. But, having helped launch a war—at last—on the proper thunderous note, TR now resigned from the Navy Department and prepared to hurl himself against the foe in person. He was not kept waiting. The War Department, which had rebuffed his scheme of leading reckless desperadoes against Mexicans, was suddenly entranced by the reservoir of ready-made soldiery conceived to be waiting on the Western plains. So was the country. In a charge,

one newspaper predicted, cowboys "would sweep every living thing before them, leaving only death and destruction in their path. They are the best shots in any country." Roosevelt was quickly invited to organize and lead a regiment of volunteer cavalry to be raised mainly in Arizona, New Mexico, Oklahoma and Indian Territory, with a small consignment of horsemen from the East.

He took over instantly, instructing War Secretary R. A. Alger to make Leonard Wood—an Army physician who had led troops against Apaches—the actual colonel of the regiment. Roosevelt did not think, he said modestly, that he could learn the intricacies of logistics and supply in much less than six weeks and did not want the time to be wasted. He would, he announced, be a lieutenant colonel. Alger agreed. However, Roosevelt was *the* Rough Rider of the Rough Riders, as the 1st U.S. Volunteer Cavalry Regiment soon became known.

Actually it was the public—or more precisely, the newspapers—that chose the name Rough Riders. Roosevelt and Wood resisted the use of the term at first, beause it lacked dignity, but when their superiors at brigade and division level started referring to the regiment as the Rough Riders in official communications, they accepted the *fait accompli.* The name had an honorable Western lineage. It had originally applied to Pony Express riders and was afterward picked up by Buffalo Bill Cody for his Wild West show horsemen, the Congress of Rough Riders of the World.

It was a fitting sobriquet for the 1st U.S. Volunteer Cavalry, because the men who flocked to San Antonio, Texas, to join the regiment represented virtually all of the archetypal characters who had played roles in the history and legend of the Old West. Their numbers included, as Roosevelt observed, "grim hunters of the mountains" and "wild riders of the plains." Cowboys were there in abundance of course, but there were in addition "men who had won fame as Rocky Mountain stage-drivers," others "who had spent endless days guiding slow wagon-trains across the grassy plains," and prospectors "who knew every camp from the Yukon to Leadville."

Professional gamblers enlisted, as did at least four frontier preachers, who "proved first-class fighters."

There were lawmen—including a marshal from infamous Dodge City, Kansas, who had lost half an ear while arresting a brawler with carnivorous instincts and sharp teeth, a deputy marshal from equally notorious Cripple Creek, Colorado, and a strong contingent of Texas Rangers. And there were outlaws, or, as Roosevelt preferred to describe them, "men whose lives in the past had not been free from the taint of those fierce kinds of crime into which the lawless spirits who dwell on the border-land between civilization and savagery so readily drift."

There were men who had fought Indians—extroopers from the regular cavalry who had battled in campaigns against Apaches and Cheyennes—and there were also Indians, Roosevelt apparently finding it possible to subjugate his "good Indian/dead Indian" attitude to his respect for fighting skills, especially when they were to be employed on his side. Approxi-

Lieutenant Colonel Roosevelt (*foreground, right*) at their Texas camp in May 1898. Roosevelt called them "a splendid set of men."

mately 20 Indians joined the regiment and "they all lived on terms of complete equality," Roosevelt observed, with their white comrades. They included a descendant of Chickasaw chiefs and a Cherokee who explained to Roosevelt that he could not be content staying at home because his "people always had fought when there was a war." One Pawnee trooper, Roosevelt noted with surprise, even possessed a sense of humor; asking for a haircut, the man explained: "Don't want to wear my hair long like a wild Indian when I'm in civilized warfare."

"They were a splendid set of men," Roosevelt said of the Rough Riders, "tall and sinewy, with resolute, weather-beaten faces, and eyes that looked a man straight in the face without flinching." They were "soldiers ready made, as far as concerned their capacity as individual fighters. What was necessary was to teach them to act together and to obey orders."

These rough-hewn Western individualists did not adjust easily, in many cases, to the niceties of military drill and discipline. An Oklahoma broncobuster named McGinty opined, when reprimanded for failing to keep in step while marching, that he was "pretty sure he could keep step on horseback." A mess steward cheerfully announced dinner to Colonel Wood and three majors with the observation, "If you fellers don't come soon, everything'll get cold," but just as cheerfully expressed himself in more conventional military terms when the proper form was explained to him. His egalitarian familiarity was surpassed by that of a recruit from Indian Territory who invaded Colonel Wood's tent after one day in camp. "Well, Colonel," he said, "I want to shake hands and say we're with you. We didn't know how we would like you fellers at first; but you're all right and you know your business and you can count on us every time!"

But the Rough Riders' hardihood and horsemanship compensated for their disregard of military convention. Many of the regiment's mounts were delivered—unshod and unridden—straight from the range. "Half the horses bucked," said Roosevelt, "but we had abundance of men utterly unmoved by any antic a horse might commit. Every animal was speedily mastered."

The public clamored for news of the Rough Riders during their four weeks of training at San Antonio, and Roosevelt seldom failed to figure prominently in the stories. Wood, noted the New York *Press,* "is lost sight of entirely in the effulgence of Teethadore." So were two other hastily organized Western cavalry outfits, Torrey's Rocky Mountain Riders and Grigsby's Cowboys, which languished at camps in Chickamauga and Jacksonville during the War and were speedily forgotten by history.

The Rough Riders got the best of everything, thanks to Roosevelt's energy, leverage in Washington, and high-handed way with bureaucrats: Krag Jorgensen carbines with smokeless ammunition rather than heavier Springfields and black powder cartridges, revolvers rather than sabers, and uniforms of lightweight brown canvas rather than the heavy blue material in which Regulars were to swelter in Cuba. And TR got his men more distinctive items: slouch hats and bright blue polka-dotted handkerchiefs to tie around their necks—a touch of costuming that made them look, he noted with pride, "exactly as a body of cowboy cavalry should look."

He got them a ship for Cuba, as well, when they reached Tampa, Florida, after a boisterous journey by rail—during which "Teddy's Terrors" were cheered by thousands along the tracks and Teddy himself passed the time reading Demolins' *Superiorité des Anglo Saxons* and grinding his teeth at the author's assumption that militarism deadened individual will. Roosevelt's own will was only stimulated as he became aware of the wild confusion amid which the Army was trying to embark its 17,000-man expeditionary force from Tampa's crowded single pier. The regiment was ordered to abandon almost all its horses, 440 of its 1,000 men, and two mascots—a young mountain lion from Arizona and an eagle from New Mexico—and Roosevelt was mortally afraid that he and the remaining 560 men would "miss the fun" in Cuba, as well.

He commandeered an empty coal train to get his soldiers to the waterfront, and then, on discovering that the transport U.S.S. *Yucatan* had been assigned to two regiments of infantry as well as to his own troopers, blocked her gangway with Rough Riders and got all his men aboard before the hapless foot soldiers realized that they were being left to wait still longer in the blazing sun.

The overcrowded transports lay sweltering at anchor for six days in Tampa harbor—a "sewer," Roosevelt raged in a letter to Henry Cabot Lodge—before finally putting to sea. Many of the men from the landlocked reaches of the West had never seen an ocean before. One who went swimming over the side was surprised to discover that the water was salty and not drinkable. Another, who had never set eyes on a body of water wider than the upper Rio Grande, complained that his hat, taken by a gust of wind, had blown "into the creek." The Westerners adapted themselves to the seafaring life by huddling in groups, as if around prairie campfires, to swap familiar tales. "They told stories of their past," Roosevelt said, "stories of the mining-camps, and the cattle-ranges, of hunting bear and deer, of war trails against the Indians, of lawless deeds of violence, of brawls in saloons, of shrewd deals in cattle and sheep, of nameless heroes—masters of men and tamers of horses."

They stayed within plain sight of Cuba's northern coast during a long, slow voyage to the island's eastern tip. The whole force was vulnerable to attack for the better part of a week as animals and men were put ashore on beaches at the hamlets of Siboney and Daiquiri (which was not yet celebrated by American cocktail drinkers) a few miles east of the objective, the harbor city of Santiago.

Roosevelt was able to get his men landed early, by borrowing a pilot from an escorting Naval vessel and insisting that the *Yucatan* steam close to the beach while others stayed timorously offshore. But deck hands drowned one of his two horses on lowering it into the water, and after getting ashore the Rough Riders, like most of the other troops, had little with which to sustain themselves but rifles and blanket rolls. Roosevelt had ordered a dozen pairs of steel-rimmed spectacles in the United States and had three of them sewn into the lining of his hat and the others stuffed into his pockets — thus ensuring clear view of the enemy — but for many days he had no razor, no spare clothing and very little food.

The confusion had only begun. Dispassionate critics of what U.S. Ambassador to England John Hay called "the splendid little war" in Cuba have long since concluded that it ended in quick victory only because the Spanish forces managed to make more mistakes than the invaders from the north. But one is left to wonder how any body of soldiery could have proceeded to battle in more inefficient fashion than the expedition from the United States.

The commander, Major General William Rufus Shafter, was saddled with much of the blame for this disorder — which stemmed largely from the War Department in Washington — and, by many, for a certain lack of zeal. Roosevelt called him "panic struck." Worse yet for his reputation, he was irritated by reporters, even such lordly creatures as Richard Harding Davis, the internationally celebrated correspondent of the *New York Herald* and *Scribner's Magazine*, and treated them much the same way he treated mosquitoes — or company cooks. Davis sought Shafter out in an attempt to evade orders that kept newspapermen bottled up aboard the transports while the troops went ashore. "I am not," he announced, "an ordinary reporter, but a descriptive writer."

"I do not care a damn what you are," said Shafter. "I'll treat all of you alike!"

The general can be forgiven — even applauded — for these sentiments, but he was unrealistic in voicing them. The War he was preparing to fight had been all but invented by Joseph Pulitzer, publisher of the "yellow" (meaning sensational) New York *World,* and William Randolph Hearst, publisher of the even yellower New York Evening *Journal.* It was being dramatized by such swarms of reporters, photographers and artists as had never been seen on a battlefield before, and was being monitored by millions of excited Americans who could hardly wait for the next extra. Eightynine correspondents had sailed from Tampa with the expedition, but these were only a minority of the newshounds; the Army calculated that 304 were eventually on hand.

Hearst himself arrived in Cuba aboard his large steam yacht *Silvia* — which carried a darkroom and a printing press, as well as two racing ponies and a big supply of ice — and wandered about within range of Spanish rifles after the shooting had started. His was not the only well-known name. Artist Howard Chandler Christy was there. So was Roosevelt's old friend, artist Frederic Remington (to whom Hearst was purported to have earlier cabled a message that his critics never forgot: "You furnish the pictures and we'll furnish the war.") Author Stephen Crane was also on hand, as was a contingent of Englishmen bent on keeping the London papers abreast of hostilities in the Caribbean.

All of them needed heroes worthy of headlines, and Shafter's intransigence simply added to Roosevelt's attractiveness. Teddy had been introduced to every reader long since, was known as a fire-eater to all, and was not only willing to talk on any subject — including Shafter — but was delighted to cultivate any reporter who strayed within the sound of his voice. Two pioneer newsreel photographers were in Cuba with piles of odd-looking equipment because he had hustled them aboard the *Yucatan* when others had rejected them. He not only welcomed Richard Harding Davis to the Rough Riders, but on getting into action kept the correspondent at his side and had him mentioned in official dispatches for having spotted some Spaniards through a pair of field glasses.

None of this should be taken to mean that Roosevelt did not behave as rashly as he spoke, nor that his little war—nowadays often equated with comic opera—was not a harrowing and dangerous undertaking for those involved in it. The Rough Riders—largely men from the arid Southwest—were not prepared for the mid-summer humidity, lashing tropical downpours and sucking mud of Cuba. They were exposed to yellow fever and malaria borne by the mosquitoes that constantly plagued them. Their food was often execrable: hardtack soaked by rain, pork turned rotten in the sun, unground coffee beans, which had to be broken up between stones. Wounded men were left untended for long periods and tobacco was unobtainable, the Army having landed with but two days' supply. And Spanish soldiers—including sharpshooters hidden in thickets—fought with desperate bravery, no matter how badly they were led.

Roosevelt was entranced by it all. He would, he said later, "have turned from my wife's deathbed" to have been in Cuba if he had been faced with that choice. His earlier doubts about his own technical military expertise vanished. He felt himself rising "over those regular army officers like a balloon" and soon decided that he was competent to command a brigade or a division. Perhaps, all things considered, he was right; he was no mean soldier. He seemed to enjoy the sound of enemy Mausers, he inspired trust and devotion in his men, and he burned, in all moments of doubt, to attack. But he was baffled during the Rough Riders' first action—as was Leonard Wood—by a foe he could not see.

The American forces moved forward on June 24 to engage some 2,000 Spanish troops who were entrenched between the beachhead at Siboney and the city of Santiago, 16 miles away. The Rough Riders were advancing along a dim trail in the tropical forest when they were ambushed by Spaniards hidden in the undergrowth. Roosevelt said men around him "went down like ninepins" from the fire of invisible riflemen and one bullet "went through a tree behind which I stood and filled my eyes with bark." But the Rough Riders formed a ragged skirmish line, pressed stubbornly ahead for three noisy hours, broke out of the jungle at last, and—joining some regulars who had emerged by way of a nearby road—began running toward the enemy positions, yelling wildly as they did so. The Spaniards abandoned their trenches—since they assumed that the thin line of Americans were the first wave of a larger force—and departed, carrying their wounded on litters, for earthworks under construction on ridges overlooking Santiago Bay.

The Rough Riders had been hurt: eight were killed and 34 wounded. The dead were interred together the next day. "There could be no more honorable burial," said Roosevelt, "than that of these men in a common grave—Indian and cowboy, miner, packer and college athlete." (The athlete was one of the Easterners in the regiment.) The men had fought courageously. A half-Cherokee trooper named Thomas Isbell had been struck seven times in a half-hour—once in the right hip, once (a graze) in the head, twice in the left hand and three times in the neck—but had refused to leave the firing line until the seventh bullet and loss of blood compelled him to do so.

Roosevelt was in high spirits as he wrote home to report that "there was no flinching," that he was saving three empty cartridges that had been taken from a dead Spaniard as presents for the children, that he had "been sleeping on the ground and so drenched with sweat that I haven't been dry for a minute, day or night," that he was presently colonel of the regiment (Leonard Wood having been promoted to command of the brigade) and that he had led one end of the charge with a borrowed carbine—while (he pointed out triumphantly) "Shafter was not even ashore." But all this was merely prelude: ahead lay an action that was to launch Roosevelt on the road to the Presidency and give the American cowboy a place in military legend as enduring, if not quite as valid, as that won by Andy Jackson's backwoodsmen at the Battle of New Orleans. It would be celebrated—mistakenly—as the Charge up San Juan Hill.

San Juan Hill was a long, barren ridge 150 feet high that was part of the last major barrier between United States forces and the Spanish-held city of Santiago at the end of June. To the right of San Juan Hill rose a smaller knoll that would be called Kettle Hill because some heavy iron vessels used in sugar refining were found on its summit. Spanish men and guns were well dug in on both heights. Five hundred yards of open savanna lay between these hills and the tropical forest

As a regimental commander in the war with Spain, Teddy wore a battered campaign hat with Rough Rider regalia, which included the U.S. Volunteers' monogram and crossed-sabers cavalry insignia.

In this painting, *Charge of the Rough Riders at San Juan Hill,* Frederic Remington perpetuated a misconception. Actually, Roosevelt

—on horseback at left—led troops up nearby Kettle Hill. Teddy acknowledged that the portrayal "was foreign to my actual conduct."

Singing the glory of a scrappy hero

You bet Ted is a fighting man
And he never cares a Rap
How big they come or little
If they're looking for a scrap

At the turn of the century, lines like these from the popular song "Oh You Teddy!" *(below right)* and other lyrics in praise of Teddy Roosevelt and his Rough Riders flowed freely from the singing throats of a hero-hungry nation.

The songwriters made Roosevelt charging up a Cuban hillside sound like a modern-day Hannibal leading his troops over the Alps, and fueled the feisty warrior's popularity. "We'll follow him to blazes, Our little Theodore," declared a line from "Teddy! Teddy! Rough and Ready!" *(opposite)*. By the time "Teddy Our Hero" *(below)* was published in 1903, the Harvard-educated cowpoke from New York had charged, sword-drawn, from the pages of America's sheet music into the lofty office of the Presidency.

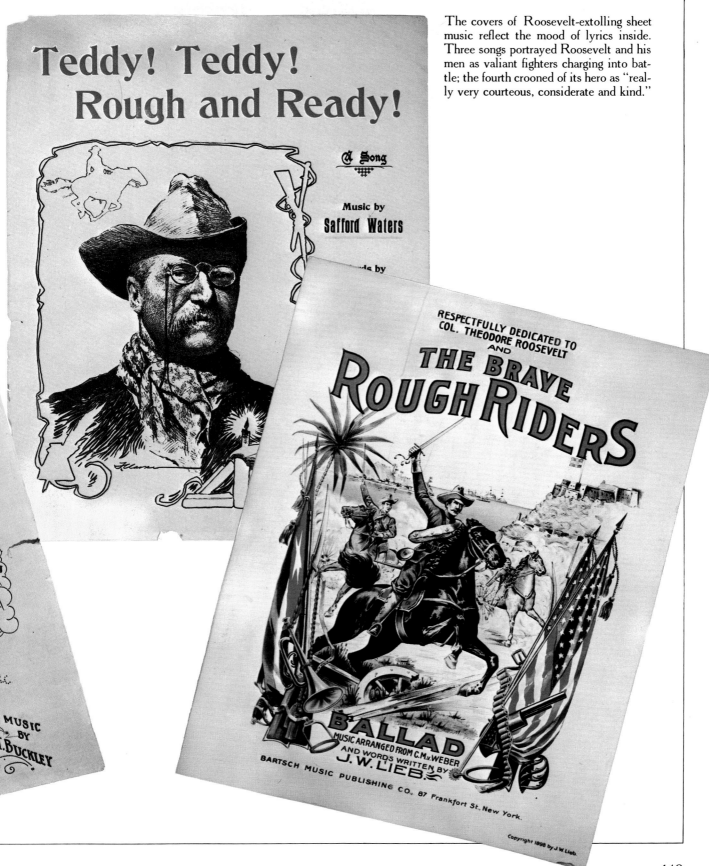

The covers of Roosevelt-extolling sheet music reflect the mood of lyrics inside. Three songs portrayed Roosevelt and his men as valiant fighters charging into battle; the fourth crooned of its hero as "really very courteous, considerate and kind."

"It seemed absurd," wrote Roosevelt *(center)* of this 1903 Colorado repast, "to get off and eat at a chuck wagon in a top hat and frock coat." But the President's hosts insisted, and "I finally did."

der of San Juan Hill itself where he found the defenders already taking to their heels. The battle for the main ridge had produced its own contingent of heroes: included among them were Lieutenant John Henry Parker, who covered the American advance by spraying the Spanish trenches with a battery of three Gatling guns, and Lieutenant Jules Ord, who led attacking infantrymen up the slope only to be killed as he became the first man to reach the top. But none of them could compete with Teddy and his bold warriors for newspaper space in the extras back home.

One hill sounded very much like another to people reading excited accounts of American victory. Correspondents were delighted to report Roosevelt's "putting spurs to his horse," and some reports seemed to suggest that the colonel of the Rough Riders had overawed the benighted Spaniards by sheer force of personality.

Roosevelt had a way of keeping himself in the news, moreover, while higher-ranking regulars faded into obscurity. He used the Associated Press to expose the fever and bad food that were the lot of soldiers in Cuba and bludgeoned the War Department—as career officers dared not—into bringing the Rough Riders home posthaste. And he became a magnet for reporters when the Riders came ashore to make camp at Long Island's Montauk Point. After they finally got their horses back, the Westerners entertained guests with rodeo stunts and basked in the approbation of visitors who came out from the city to admire them. Emotion ran high when they were mustered out of service there on September 15, having been in existence for less than five months. Roosevelt was presented with a small bronze statue of a broncobuster by Frederic Remington as a token of the Rough Riders' "love and esteem" and asked for the "privilege" of shaking each man's hand. Many in the line of troopers wept as they filed past to say goodbye.

They were not, as events quickly began to prove, being mustered out of the public mind. Roosevelt celebrated them all over again—and, by implication, himself—with *The Rough Riders,* a book issued in 1899 after running serially in *Scribner's Magazine.* The author received a good deal of indignant mail, for he had taken to referring to The San Juan Hills in plural, thus giving Kettle Hill a topographical impor-

tance his critics felt it lacked, and seemed to be suggesting—though he did so modestly—that he might have been first of all Americans to burst into a Spanish trench. Columnist Finley Peter Dunne's famed Mr. Dooley suggested alternate titles: *Alone in Cubia, Th' Biography iv a Hero be Wan who Knows,* or *Th' Darin' Exploits iv a Brave Man be an Actual Eye Witness.*

But the general public, and certainly the voters of New York state, applauded. Roosevelt campaigned for the governorship in the fall of 1898 with an "honor guard" of uniformed Rough Riders, including a trumpeter who sounded stirring bugle calls and won the election. The Republicans could not leave so intriguing a hero long in Albany; he was elected to the Vice Presidency on William McKinley's ticket in 1900, became President when McKinley was assassinated in 1901, was elected in his own right by a huge majority in 1904—and celebrated this public approval of his belligerent politics and personal charm by bringing an honor guard of Rough Riders to Washington for his inauguration.

The United States emerged as a world power of the first rank during his years as President, in no small part because he exercised his imperialistic views—which he defined as expressions of "fundamental frontier virtues"—in American foreign policy. "These qualities, derived from the pioneers, were not confined to the pioneers," he wrote. "They are shown in the deeds of the nation," and were exemplified, in his mind, by "two great feats" during his time in office: his sending the United States "Great White Fleet" around the world—to show foreigners its guns like a Western lawman strolling through a noisy saloon—and his creation of the Panama Canal.

He was certain that he was behaving in the best traditions of the old frontier when he bludgeoned his way past certain legal difficulties in gaining a right-of-way for the Canal. The Isthmus of Panama was part of Colombia, and the Colombians objected to his grand scheme. "We may," he said, drawing on his ever-ready Western imagery, "have to give a lesson to those jackrabbits," and did so, forthwith, by implicitly supporting a coup d'état in which Panamanians severed the Isthmus from Colombian control while American battleships lay significantly offshore. "I took the canal and let

Congress debate," he said, "and while the debate goes on the canal does also."

Roosevelt resorted to what came to be called his "Western analogy" again in refusing to countenance guerrillas under Emilio Aguinaldo when they strove to gain control of the Philippines, which the United States had taken as a prize of victory in the Spanish-American War. To have done so, he said, would have been "like granting self government to an Apache reservation under some local chief." Maintaining United States garrisons in the Philippines was no different than "sending soldiers to South Dakota in 1890 during the Ogillallah outbreak. The reasoning which justifies our having made war against Sitting Bull also justifies our having checked the outbreaks of Aguinaldo and his followers."

He made this philosophy a central theme of foreign policy in a larger sense. "Every expansion of a civilized power is a conquest for peace," he said. "Whether the barbarian be the Red Indian on the frontier of the United States" or "the Afghan on the border of British India, the result is the same. In the long run civilized man finds he can keep the peace only by subduing his barbarian neighbor."

Most Americans applauded, though Roosevelt did not lack critics. And they applauded his application of frontier concepts to domestic problems as well. People in populous Eastern states were increasingly troubled by the difficulties of their new, technological age: by urban crowding, which threatened their sense of identity, by the monotony of repetitive work in big factories, by resentment, even a kind of helplessness in the face of huge trusts, which seemed to be quasi governments of their own. Roosevelt seemed to offer them alternatives with his talk of frontier equality and frontier virtues—the legacies, he said, of all Americans, even those who had never seen the West—and by the vigor with which he attacked the trusts, stared down kaisers and kings and shared his confidence in the future of a nation blessed by Western ideals.

He was as intent on preserving the resources and the beauty of the real West—that actual geographical region that still stretched from the Mississippi to the Pacific, even if it was no longer inhabited by pioneers and gunfighters—as he was on preserving the virtues of the Old West. One of his biographers said that in terms of conservation his years in the White House were "such an era of enlightenment as the nation had never before experienced."

More than a million acres—most of them in the West—were added to the national park system during Roosevelt's administration. He oversaw the creation of 51 wildlife refuges and set aside 16 areas of special natural beauty as national monuments, including Muir Woods in California and Devil's Tower in Wyoming. He curbed the reckless exploitation of forests in the West by instituting selective cutting. "Conservation means development as much as it does protection," he said. He worked tirelessly for reclamation schemes, with the result that 30 big irrigation projects were started during his administration.

Roosevelt reserved his deepest emotional commitment for the Westerners with whom he had hunted and gone to war. He eagerly anticipated receiving, in the White House, letters from a New Mexico attorney and former Rough Rider who kept him abreast of all the misdeeds of these tough hombres who had served under him in Cuba: "I have the honor to report that Comrade Ritchie, late of Troop G is in jail at Trinidad, Colorado on a charge of murder. Comrade Webb, late of Troop D, has just killed two men at Bisbee, Arizona." Roosevelt could storm at the crimes of anarchists and corrupt politicians, but he tended to chuckle at shooting scrapes by his former soldiers and devoted himself as assiduously to finding employment for them as for all Rough Riders down on their luck—including a post as warden of the Arizona territorial penitentiary for ex-Sergeant Benjamin Daniels, who had just been released from the place after he served a term for homicide.

Friends from ranching days—"with whom I had eaten at the tail-board of a chuck wagon"—were equally important to him and were welcomed to the White House whenever they appeared in Washington. One of them, "a huge powerful man who had a fighting character," was invited to join Roosevelt and the British Ambassador for lunch. "Remember, Jim," Roosevelt said solemnly just before they entered the White House dining room, "that if you shot at the feet of the British ambassador to make him dance, it would be likely to cause international complications." The Westerner, said Roosevelt, "responded with unaffect-

ed horror: 'Why, Colonel, I shouldn't think of it, I shouldn't think of it!' "

Roosevelt seemed certain that he was retiring from politics when he left the White House in 1909. He was exasperated, however, by William Howard Taft's insistence on running the country his own way rather than the Roosevelt way, and he led other dissenting Republicans off into a splinter Bull Moose Party and tried for the Presidency again in 1912. He failed, splitting the G.O.P. vote and opening the doors of the White House to Woodrow Wilson. He remained a public figure. He gave speeches, he wrote opinionated articles, hunted African big game and explored the jungles of South America. He burned to lead a division of U.S. volunteers to Europe when the United States entered World War I and asked Wilson, in impas-

sioned tones, to let him do so. It was a romantic proposal by a warrior long past his prime. Wilson refused (though not before France's Premier Georges Clemenceau wrote to say that French soldiers were asking, "But where is Roosevelt?").

His youngest son, Quentin, was killed in France in July 1918. Roosevelt—who was to die himself, of a coronary embolism, less than six months afterward—clung, when informed of the news, to the philosophy he had formed on the Little Missouri River so many years before. He seemed to be saluting the companions of his youth on the prairies in addition to his son when he responded with his last published words: "Only those are fit to live who do not fear to die; and none are fit to die who have shrunk from the joy of life. Both life and death are parts of the same Great Adventure."

Guardian of the heritage of beauty

"Leave it as it is," said President Roosevelt, looking out over the Grand Canyon in 1903. "You cannot improve on it. Keep it for your children, your children's children, and for all who come after you."

Americans with an expansionist heritage and vistas of seemingly endless encroachable space were hardly inclined to leave the West as it was. But Roosevelt, as both a private citizen and President, attacked the issue with characteristic determination and helped forge into national policy his belief that "there is nothing more practical than the preservation of beauty."

Nowhere were the results more breathtaking than in the West's national parks. Yellowstone *(right)* was first to benefit, when Roosevelt helped found the Boone and Crockett Club in 1887 to campaign for more protection for the park, which was threatened by hunters and developers. The campaign led to the National Park Protective Act of 1894, which gave the conservation movement the force of law.

For Roosevelt, the Act was only a beginning. During his Presidency, five national parks were created—the same number founded under all his predecessors combined.

Roosevelt died just before the creation of Grand Canyon National Park in 1919. But the movement that began with the Boone and Crockett Club's lonely fight for Yellowstone had matured into a powerful force. Roosevelt's conservation campaign, according to one historian, was "a revolution in American life" that saved the West for future generations.

A Yellowstone geyser spews forth a spray of steaming water in this 1881 painting by Albert Bierstadt. "Yellowstone is a park for the people," wrote Roosevelt, "and the representatives of the people should see that it is molested in no way."

The peaks and cathedral-scale trees of Yosemite National Park rise gracefully in Thomas Hill's 1871 painting. Roosevelt was moved by "the majestic trunks, beautiful in color and symmetry," during a 1903 trip there, and vigorously supported funds for the park's administration.

Delicately tinted mists waft around the labyrinthian forms of Arizona's Grand Canyon in this 1908 painting by Thomas Moran. Roosevelt's desire that nothing would be done "to mar the wonderful grandeur, the sublimity, the great loneliness and beauty of the canyon" was partially realized when it became a national park.

5 | A mad rush for black gold

The 1937 skyline of Oklahoma City bristles with oil derricks—incongruous architectural companions to the neoclassical state capitol.

"Everybody was just a bunch of boomers. Here today and gone tomorrow. Law and order—they didn't have it. Gambling and everything else going on." Though the words might have described any Western gold-rush town of the 1800s, the scene this time was Beaumont, Texas, the year 1901, and the mineral causing the boom was "black gold"—oil.

Equipped with drills and piping instead of picks and shovels, arriving by railroad rather than covered wagon, the fortune seekers descended on the petroleum-rich Southwest in the early 1900s in what one historian described as "a California gold rush concentrated in time and space." Even the characters were occasionally the same: W. Scott Heywood, who in earlier years had found gold in the Klondike, drilled himself a well at Beaumont that made his Alaska trek seem hardly worth the effort. The new stakes were astronomical: within a 40-mile radius of Ranger, Texas, in 1919, oil that was worth nine times the 1849 gold output of all California poured from the ground.

Like Placerville and Goldfield before them, new boomtowns with names like Batson, Ponca City and Caddo absorbed a flood of would-be millionaires, job seekers, thugs, prostitutes and gamblers. Beaumont's population jumped from 9,000 to 50,000 in just two years after its first oil well, the famed Lucas Gusher, came in. Even state capitols, like that at Oklahoma City (below), were not immune from encroaching derricks.

"We are wealthy beyond our calculations," boasted the 1901 *Beaumont Enterprise,* phrasing anew a traditional Western theme of prosperity and self-reliance. "We are independent of everybody and everything." In the oil boom, the Old West lived again.

A new boom born in a Texas gusher

Pattillo Higgins, an extraordinarily bull-headed Texan, was possessed by an extraordinary obsession: the fortune in petroleum that lay—or so he was convinced—beneath a low hill that rose above the South Texas rice country four miles south of the town of Beaumont. The peculiarities of this rise of land—which was to be celebrated around the world as Spindletop—were common knowledge. Gas and foul-smelling sulfur fumes rose from fissures in its surface. Higgins was certain that the fumes denoted oil and spent most of a decade scheming feverishly to extract the stuff.

A good deal of his reputation for sanity vanished in the process. Higgins had been a barroom brawler as a young man but had turned, on losing an arm in a logging accident, to teaching a Baptist Sunday school and to reading books on geology. He assailed various wealthy citizens of Beaumont with the smattering of scientific lore thus gained, and talked several of them into giving him financial support. They formed a company in 1892 and acquired 2,700 acres on and around the hill, but after seven years they had nothing to show for their endeavors but three dry holes.

Higgins refused to give up and, as a last, desperate device, ran an ad in a trade journal offering to share in "a great, oil bearing concession." He got only one reply, and when the interested party—one Anthony Lucas, engineer—arrived in Beaumont, Higgins had little but a tale of frustration to offer in explaining the ruling passion of his life.

But Anthony Lucas (born Luchich in Dalmatia, which at that time belonged to Austria) was immedi-

ately swept up in Higgins' obsession. He was an unusual fellow himself, with an unusual background: he had studied engineering at the Polytechnic Institute in Graz and served in the Austrian Navy before crossing the Atlantic to seek his fortune in the United States. He had designed a gang-saw for Michigan saw mills, mined gold and copper in the West and drilled for salt on the Gulf Coast.

Captain Lucas—as he styled himself, although his highest naval rank had been lieutenant—was excited by Spindletop. He had encountered traces of petroleum in Louisiana salt domes—great, cylindrical plugs of sodium chloride that had pushed their way toward the surface, through the ages, from the bed of a prehistoric sea—and believed Higgins' big mound masked a similar formation. Better yet, he had money: he handed Higgins $11,000, gave him a note for another $20,000 and guaranteed him 10 per cent of any profits from the enterprise. The new partner agreed to pay for the drilling while taking a 90 per cent interest in the venture.

Lucas erected the kind of rotary drilling rig he had utilized while seeking salt deposits in Louisiana and addressed himself to the job—which he assumed he could conclude in only a few weeks—of discovering a new oil pool. He had a considerable amount of confidence in rotary drilling, which was a relatively new development in oil exploration: a bit spinning at the end of a column of pipe would be able to drill faster and probe deeper and would allow better management of an embryo well than one that was simply raised and dropped to pound its way into the earth, as in the cable drilling method that had been used to discover oil in northern states like Pennsylvania.

But after six months of trying to penetrate the hundreds of feet of loose sand that lay under Spindletop, Lucas, too, was stony broke. He needed financial sup-

Several hours after blowing in on January 10, 1901, the Lucas Gusher at Spindletop spews a greasy black plume 200 feet into the sky, signaling what was then the greatest oil discovery in the world.

port and better equipment, and approached a flamboyant Pittsburgh speculator named James McClurg Guffey and Guffey's cautious and quiet partner, John H. Galey. The pair set conditions after Galey made a trip of inspection to Beaumont: Lucas was to buy up leases to as much acreage on and around the dome as possible, give a seven-eighths interest in the project to his rescuers, and agree that only one deep hole was to be sunk. The project was to be abandoned if this first effort failed. The captain agreed.

Guffey offered to pay him an interim salary and to reimburse him for the expenses that he had already incurred. Lucas refused, even though he and his wife, a woman whose faith equalled his own, were reduced to selling their furniture in order to put food on the table. But Guffey did get him $300,000—having borrowed the money from Andrew Mellon—and Lucas leased some 14,000 more acres and started another well forthwith.

This fifth hole at Spindletop has been characterized by experts as an "engineer's well"—one that would have been impossible to sink if Lucas had not been able to advance the state of the art in drilling it. This may

indeed be true: he devised a back pressure valve at one crucial point, thus preventing gas from hurling debris into the derrick and wrecking the operation. His drillers—Al, Curt and J. G. Hamill of Louisiana—also bequeathed subsequent oilmen an imperative new technique by pumping mud into the well to seal off loose sand and to lubricate the bit. But none of them had any premonition of incipient drama when they pulled 1,020 feet of drill pipe to replace a worn bit and began lowering it back down the hole on the morning of January 10, 1901.

They barely escaped with their lives. The well roared. It spewed mud. It hurled four tons of drilling pipe skyward, and as these lengths of broken, flying metal came clanging down it emitted gas and then showers of rocks. Finally, with a bang like the very crack of doom, it erected a towering black geyser such as the continent had never seen before. Lucas was driving toward the derrick when he saw the dark fountain rising in the distance. He whipped his horse and was careening toward the well at a gallop when he met the first of the crew. "Al!" he yelled. "Al! What is it?" "Oil, Captain," cried Al Hamill. "It's oil!" The first of Spindletop's sightseers—neighboring farmers and their startled wives—came laboring into view as Lucas leaped out to hug the driller and wrestled him about in a crazy little dance.

Thus began—at a time when the Old West was being consigned to history books and popular entertainment—the biggest, wildest boom the West had ever experienced. Forty thousand people descended on Beaumont in the next few hectic months. They came looking for a new kind of job, a new kind of adventure and even, it seemed to most of them, a new kind of money, since it was spent so casually and gambled so feverishly by those who breathed the town's oil-tainted air. Country boys—or boll weevils as more practiced oil-field hands called them—rode freight trains toward Spindletop by the hundreds to seek work on oil rigs. Bankers, lease traders and bunco artists hurried to Beaumont, too, and so did teamsters, gunmen, cardsharps, prostitutes, wildcatters large and small and seers bent on "witching" out underground fortunes with peach twigs.

The sleepy town on the Neches River was as unprepared for them as it was for excursion trains full of

Pattillo Higgins, first to be convinced that there was oil under Spindletop, wanted the discovery to be called the Beaumont Oil Field and he put that name on his calling card. But "Spindletop" prevailed.

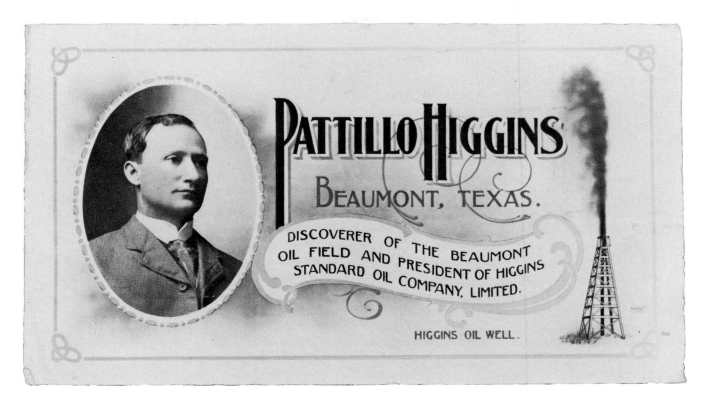

PATTILLO HIGGINS

BEAUMONT, TEXAS.

DISCOVERER OF THE BEAUMONT OIL FIELD AND PRESIDENT OF HIGGINS STANDARD OIL COMPANY, LIMITED.

HIGGINS OIL WELL.

rubbernecks bent on seeing a gusher, or for the forest of wooden derricks that soon rose on its outskirts. Five hundred fly-by-night oil companies suddenly materialized, many of them with no more excuse for existence than a lease on a few square feet of ground. Newcomers were drawn into a feverish trade in stock certificates that promised sudden wealth. Actual land brought astronomical prices: from $200,000 to nearly one million dollars an acre within the "proved area," tapering down to $1,000 for outlying acres up to 150 miles away. Traders carried suitcases full of cash while they dickered for leases on tiny scraps of land that were overlooked by bigger operators—leases that occasionally rose a hundred times in value in hours. Water could be purchased for five cents a cup, and silver dollars were imported by the freight carload to bolster the money supply of the town.

Sleeping accommodation was at a premium. The well-heeled found beds by taking trains to Houston in order to return by sleeper overnight to Beaumont. The less fortunate rented barber chairs, billiard tables, loft space in livery stables or six-hour occupancy of cots that were jammed into the city auditorium.

The law went largely ignored: "humanity," as one early arrival put it, "was plumb tore up." Victims of holdup men, or of bartenders who slipped knockout drops to the prosperous, were discovered floating at dawn in the muddy Neches River. "There was eleven men killed on my beat in nine months," remembered Will Armstrong, one of the hard-pressed policemen of Beaumont. "One of them had been looking in a window at a bartender counting his money. The bartender picked up a little gun, shot the man and went right on counting."

But the boom that was set off by Higgins' obsession and Lucas' innovative engineering reached far beyond the environs of Beaumont. Spindletop's gusher started to change the concepts, the practices and, indeed, the very structure of the United States oil industry from the moment it blew in. Salt domes similar to the one that formed the hill from which it sprang were common along the Gulf Coast; however, they had been ignored by oil seekers because they bore no relation to the geology of earlier fields in Pennsylvania and Ohio—areas where petroleum was mostly contained in shallow sands or porous limestone.

165

The Lucas well not only demonstrated that gas and oil were frequently trapped on the tops or flanks of such salt-dome formations, but also proved that the Southwest harbored subterranean reservoirs of petroleum that were far greater than any that had been tapped in 40 years of drilling in the Northern states. The first six wells drilled at Spindletop produced, among them, more petroleum per day than all the other oil wells then known in the world.

John D. Rockefeller's Standard Oil Company had monopolized the United States oil business before 1901 and had cornered most world markets for kerosene-lamp fuel, its principal product. The monopoly (at least in production) was broken by the gusher at Spindletop, not only because the pool beneath the dome was so enormous, but because the discovery of petroleum in such unexpected circumstances inspired a stampede of entrepreneurs—some well-financed, others lone wildcatters operating on hopes, lies and a little borrowed money—who found even bigger fields and started oil companies of their own. And this great Western oil rush occurred at the very time that the rapidly proliferating automobile provided a soaring new demand for petroleum (178 factories were producing cars by 1904, and by

1915 Henry Ford alone had sold half a million of the gasoline-burning machines).

Oil, like gold, the wildcatters believed, was where you found it, and the era of exploration inspired by Spindletop's black geyser was dramatized by strikes whose names still echo away in the history of the West: Glenn Pool, Indian Territory, 1905; Cushing Field, Oklahoma—with its satellite towns of Drumright, Dropright, Alright and Damnright—1912; El Dorado, Kansas, 1915; Ranger, Texas, 1917; Desdemona (formerly Hogtown) and Burkburnett, Texas, 1918; Ponca City, Oklahoma, 1918; Mexia, Texas, 1920; Signal Hill at Long Beach, California, 1921; Seminole, Oklahoma, 1926; and the East Texas Field, 1930. These oil rushes inspired a kind of regeneration of the Old West, spawned boomtowns fully as noisy and dangerous as any mining camp or trail town of the past, and not only revived but often magnified that faith in individualism and those risks and expectations that in an earlier era had characterized life on the frontier.

Spindletop's original prophet, Pattillo Higgins, was all but forgotten in the frenzied boom that his stubbornness had engendered. He ended up with only one tenth of Captain Lucas' one-eighth interest in Guffey's and Galey's enterprise, and he spent the money drilling more wells. Every one of them, like his first three at Spindletop, was a dry hole. Lucas settled for $400,000 in cash—only a fragment of the fortunes he helped to create, but enough to allow him to retreat to Washington, D.C., and to listen in quiet and contentment to the reverberations from his historic accomplishment at Beaumont. But he engaged, before leaving, in a final, frantic struggle with the monster he had contrived at Spindletop.

The great gusher spouted 100,000 barrels a day before the Hamill brothers finally managed, after nine days, to shut it down. Lucas drove his buggy around the rice country, hiring farmers and some 40 four-horse teams he used to build dikes around a rising lagoon of oil. He saved a large portion of it. A spark from a passing locomotive set the lake on fire. He started counter-fires and the two great curtains of flame extinguished each other on meeting—"while the earth trembled," as he noted in a report, "as if shaken by an earthquake."

The Spindletop oil rush, like the whole Western boom that followed it, was an exercise in wastefulness as well as gunplay and dubious speculation—a wastefulness dictated, in no small part, by the "rule of capture," a concept in English common law that the Supreme Court of Pennsylvania utilized in 1889 as a means of establishing the ownership of petroleum beneath American ground. The court decided that oil, like wild game, belonged to the man who bagged it on his own property even if he drew upon reserves that lay under someone else's land.

Derricks at Beaumont rose within a few feet of each other as every man labored to get rich before the supply ran out. At Spindletop 440 wells were sunk in the first year and within six years the gas pressure that forced oil to the surface was exhausted. The field stopped producing. "The cow," remarked Lucas sadly when he visited Spindletop some years later, "was milked too hard."

The passing of the field was little mourned by brigades of "doodlebuggers"—pseudo-scientific diviners and mystics—who materialized as if by magic, promising new Spindletops bigger than the first. Some professed supernatural gifts, others claimed secret scientific knowledge, and all were prepared to lead promoters and drillers to oil. A good many of them prospered, for a seer or diviner with a reputation supplied the bemused wildcatter with faith, and wildcatters stubborn enough to drill on locations ignored by others hit oil repeatedly during the early years in the Southwest. Doodlebuggers, in fact—thanks to the laws of chance, the era's imperfect understanding of underground structures, and the widespread presence of petroleum in Texas and Oklahoma—discovered much more oil than geologists in the period of feverish exploration after Spindletop.

The oil seekers presented themselves in infinite variety. "Jumpers" professed to feel pain, usually in the soles of their feet, when traversing ground beneath which petroleum lay concealed. Their cries of agony were calculated to convince the most cynical observer. "Trompers" experienced no physical reaction but claimed that they found themselves making deepening footprints as they walked over a likely location. Some of these self-appointed guides proclaimed themselves the possessors of extraordinary vision: one charlatan toured the oil fields with a small black boy who would occasionally intone, while peering into a length of stovepipe aimed at the ground, "I see something dark and a-flowing." "Witchers" who had reputations for finding underground water with a forked tree branch switched to oil seeking, too—often after tying a small bottle of crude to their chosen twig to sensitize it to its new task.

But doodlebuggers quickly armed themselves with more impressive equipment—machines that boasted batteries, coils, antennae and flashing lights or electric bells—and talked learnedly of "sine waves" and the detection of "effluvium" drawn upward by the "porosity of the earth." A large number of these charlatans were unmasked, including an Englishman who claimed to have been a member of the Royal Geological Survey of India and employed a device that fired off showers of sparks whenever he slyly moved a ring (as his critics finally discovered) on one leg of its tripod. However, there were clairvoyants, like Annie Jackson of Corsicana, Texas, who believed, quite genuinely, in their own powers and used these powers only when wildcatters called on them to seek advice. A Colonel A. E. Humphreys, discoverer of the field at Mexia,

gave Annie $8,500 after he drilled a producing well on a farm that was owned by a man in whose palm she had "seen oil."

None of these clairvoyants seemed to be as gifted or as innocent, however, as a 13-year-old named Guy Findley, who was taken by promoters to the country near Beaumont—along with his brother, an attorney, who was acting as an intermediary—to locate oil for them following the Spindletop strike. Guy had discovered in himself a "feeling" for underground water and had demonstrated it over and over

since the age of 10. He pointed out a location in which he believed that oil would be found, but the promoters fell out with his brother over money, and Guy, deciding that he was commercializing "communion with the Deity," returned to his father's ranch near Uvalde. Oil was later discovered on the spot he had designated and following that Guy was celebrated throughout Texas as "The X-Ray-Eyed Boy." He continued to locate water to help others, but thought that his gift had been damaged by greed and never again consented to hunt for petroleum.

This forest of derricks sprang up alongside Spindletop's Boiler Avenue when speculators divided tracts into pieces as small as one thirty-second of an acre and sold them to drillers. The inefficient spacing of wells soon exhausted Spindletop's profitability.

But wildcatters, not mystics, kept the Western oil boom alive after Spindletop. "Some fellow that hasn't got a dollar is always ready to enter into a contract to drill a well for somebody," said a wildcatter named L. L. James. "And then he hopes to go out and rent his rig on a credit and pay for it with bottom-hole money and hire his crew and buy his fuel oil and his derrick and all that, all on the credit, hoping that he'll luck out. Sometimes they do and most of the time they didn't because they just couldn't do it. They got too deep in debt before they got the well completed."

Fate responded to wildcatters with maddening contrariety. There were drillers who spent their entire lives sinking wells that were within yards of vast fortunes with no return whatsoever, entrepreneurs who seemed to be guided to oil by some unerring species of intuition—until their luck failed—and a rare minority who parlayed underground discoveries into great oil companies of their own and went on getting richer until the day they died.

There were also those like S. L. Fowler, a Texas cotton farmer who became a wildcatter simply to placate his wife. Mrs. Fowler was convinced that there was oil under the back forty and refused to let her husband sell the property and go into cattle ranching until he proved her wrong. Fowler lacked the money to drill and so went to his neighbors with a share-the-wealth proposal. "Well," as one of them later recalled, "there was nothing particularly favorable to encourage anyone to want to spend any money or time or effort on the Fowler land. So we sat around and decided that just as friends and neighbors, we'd just do our Boy Scout turn by putting in a little, not enough to hurt any of us, but maybe enough to poor-boy a well down."

Fowler needed $12,000 to sink a well deep enough to satisfy his wife; he had $1,000 and the neighbors produced the remainder. They chose a spot "right north of the hog pen." It proved providential. They discovered the giant Burkburnett Field—though they would have hit salt water had they drilled only a little distance away. The Fowler Farm Oil Company sold out for $18 million a few months later. Every $100 of the neighbors' pool repaid its investor 150 times over.

Wildcatters were creatures of chance, but none gambled with more confidence nor ladled out the rewards of good fortune as lavishly as Ernest Whitworth Marland, the most flamboyant of the high rollers who got rich in Oklahoma. Marland seemed miscast amid the roughnecks of the big boom; his father, a wealthy Pennsylvanian, had sent him to a Tennessee preparatory school run by Thomas Hughes, author of *Tom Brown's School Days,* and then to law classes in Michigan, in the hopes of making him a statesman. The youth spoke, dressed and behaved like a gentleman and developed a heady set of social aspirations during his

years as a student. But he discovered poker as well, spent all his spare time perfecting his game and thirsted for similarly risky activity when he emerged into the world of men.

He found it immediately. He began dealing in West Virginia oil leases, made a million dollars in a few months, lost it all in a few more, borrowed train fare and headed for Oklahoma—drawn by tales of the discovery of the fabulous Glenn Pool. There he rubbed shoulders with cowboys and roustabouts and demonstrated a "nose for oil" that was to make him one of the wonders of the Southwest. He hit it rich after talking a Ponca chieftain into letting him drill into an Indian burial mound, then bid for more Indian leases with a recklessness bigger operators would not match. In a single day he contributed $2,477,300 to the Osage tribe. He opened six fields in quick succession and found himself, after two wild decades, the owner of a company that had 600 service stations and sold petroleum products in every state and 17 foreign countries.

Marland spent money as if he owned John D. Rockefeller's oil as well. He paid his employees princely

salaries and provided them with life, health and accident insurance as well as free medical and dental care. He threw up free houses for 200 of them on pleasant, one-acre tracts. He contributed money to churches, orphanages and hospitals with one hand while, with the other, he built himself a mansion fit for an earl on a 400-acre estate at Ponca City and equipped himself with a yacht, a private railroad car and a plantation in Mississippi.

He organized and accoutered a polo team and, having thus introduced an elevated purview of sport to Oklahoma, assembled a pack of hounds and a stable of hunters and sent his rough-hewn compatriots hallooing off across coyote country after a specially imported English fox. The fox emerged the winner; it eluded the hounds, circled back to the automobile in which it had been delivered, and was eventually discovered on the car's front seat awaiting return transportation to the United Kingdom.

Marland's exuberance led him, in the end, to ruin. J. P. Morgan and Company swallowed him up when petroleum prices dropped in 1927 and then spit him

out, his fortune drained away, in 1928. But he was far from defeated. He got himself elected governor of Oklahoma and spent public money on aid for schools, flood control, new highways and old-age pensions with the same fervor he had earlier displayed spending his own. The capitol in Oklahoma City was surrounded by privately owned oil wells draining off riches that, Marland felt, belonged to the state. He responded by leasing the capitol grounds to the highest bidder and permitting oil rigs to be erected near the executive mansion. The public was outraged and Marland called out the National Guard to stave off protesters. The state treasury profited handsomely but Marland was not reelected. He retreated to a small house on a corner of his one-time estate at Ponca City and died there, a poor man, in 1941.

Not so Harry Sinclair, another early promoter who accumulated vast wealth after winning a first million by hunch drilling in the Southwest. Sinclair, a one-time pharmacist from Independence, Kansas, was small (Napoleonic, feature writers would say later), wore silk underwear and had some of Marland's instinct for

self-indulgence and the sporting life: he was to finance a baseball team in the outlaw Federal League in 1914 and would win the Kentucky Derby with a thorough-bred named Zev in 1923. He was a man born to succeed. He had a disciplined and orderly mind as well as a bent for intrigue, a certain natural rapacity and a compulsion—never quite satisfied—to be bigger than John D. Rockefeller.

Sinclair was hunting for drilling sites on Indian lands, like all the other speculators in northeastern Oklahoma, when he materialized in Tulsa in 1905. He seemed unique even so. He had staked himself for the fray by unusual means—collecting insurance money for shooting off one of his own toes. His capacity for a labyrinthian method was revealed more clearly, however, after he set out—through the offices of a front man named W. J. Connelly—to lease 110 promising acres in Indian territory from a Cherokee youth named Frank Tanner.

This task was complicated by the fact that Tanner, a minor, had already leased the ground to others through the offices of the Department of the Interior.

Sinclair was stimulated by the challenge. He knew that the government would cease acting as the Indian boy's agent on his 21st birthday, the lease would then become invalid on that date—February 14, 1908—and the man who leaped in before the original investors had a chance to renegotiate the deal would have drilling privileges on land that was close to a new strike near the Kansas border. He sent Connelly to promise Tanner a $20,000 bonus—money Sinclair did not actually possess.

When Sinclair discovered that the youth fancied himself a baseball player, he told Connelly to sign him up as a pitcher for the hometown team back in Independence. Connelly, who decided that Tanner still seemed "nervous," then topped this offer by persuading the manager of the Pittsburgh Pirates—an old friend—to send him a letter offering Tanner a tryout in the spring of 1908.

Disaster yawned, nevertheless. Tanner disappeared a few days before the crucial date and Connelly, hot on the trail, discovered that he had been seen in Oklahoma City with another canny oilman, Charles J. Wrightsman, and an associate, Gene Blaize. Connelly called a friend in Oklahoma City by telephone and asked him to keep the quarry in sight. This proved hard on the friend: the rival oilmen talked the police into throwing him into jail after they became aware of his surveillance. Connelly puffed into town the next day and located the hotel in which his antagonists were staying. He cornered Tanner in a washroom, told the youth that the Pirates wanted him in Pittsburgh at once, hauled him off to the railroad station and got him aboard a train.

But Connelly's triumph was short lived. Wrightsman and Blaize came hurrying into the Pullman behind him, rushed Tanner out to the platform, pushed him into a Thomas Flyer—one of the few horseless carriages in Oklahoma in 1908—and vanished with him in a cloud of dust. Connelly telephoned Sinclair, who set off for Oklahoma City posthaste to join the hunt; then Connelly started calling law officers in outlying towns to demand that the Thomas Flyer be stopped "owing to an emergency affecting one of the men in it." Night had fallen, however, before he was able to find out that the machine was parked in front of a hotel in Enid, which was 73 miles away from Oklahoma

City, and that its occupants were settled down in bed. Sinclair hired a special train, resumed the chase and, once arrived at Enid, persuaded the local chief of police to take Tanner into custody in order to separate him from his kidnappers. Sinclair then banged on Wrightsman's door and spent the rest of the night trying to argue him into a 50-50 split of the oil rights at issue. Wrightsman refused to do so—in amused and tolerant tones, as if he faced a holdup man who held a water pistol. However, he changed his mind in the morning. The police chief produced Tanner, who had been 21 years old since midnight. The Indian turned to Connelly with what seemed like relief, and said, "I want you to have my lease."

Wrightsman now insisted upon the split and Sinclair, unwilling to risk further dependence on Tanner's malleable sense of loyalty, fell in with him immediately. The pair joined forces, forthwith, in a venture they called the Chaser Oil Company, thus adding to the list of peculiarly named firms (among them the Only Oil Company, the Midnight Oil Company and the Hoppy Toad Oil Company) that bloomed during the big boom. Although Tanner was soon disabused of his hope of pitching for the Pittsburgh Pirates, he did not complain. Sinclair and Wrightsman discovered two million barrels of petroleum under his land and made him rich.

Sinclair had a connoisseur's appreciation of cunning and a talent for judging the motives of those who practiced it. He launched himself on the road to real wealth—having made his first million—by betting that a wildcat promoter named Tom Slick had stumbled over something big in drilling a well in some scrubby hill country that was 40 miles west of Tulsa, close to the town of Cushing. The well was not a big producer; however, Slick was moved to extraordinary precautions while grabbing leases around it after it came in. He reduced the mobility of other leasers by renting every horse and buggy in Cushing's livery stables for 10 days, and denied them the opportunity of validating contracts, in the event any of them proved willing to invade the surrounding countryside on foot, by hiring the services of every notary in town for the same period of time.

A map of the area disclosed that Creek Indian lands were lying unclaimed amid Slick's widening patchwork

This portable jail cell awaits delivery from Houston to a Texas oil boomtown. The hasty growth of oil towns left no time to construct jails for the unsavory characters who migrated in droves to any new strike.

In Batson, Texas, where not even a spare portable cell was available, a prisoner *(below)* is secured by a more primitive method. Drunks were chained just long enough for a tree-side nap, then were released.

During an oil rush in 1927, wagons crowd Seminole, Oklahoma. The muddy streets of the town invited humor: in one story a man

whose head scarcely showed above the muck was offered a hand up to the sidewalk. "No thanks," he responded, "I'm on horseback."

Automobiles and wagons crowd Burkburnett, Texas, which boasted 56 oil wells three weeks after its 1918 strike. Hollywood film makers later chose this city as the location for the movie *Boom Town*.

of leased acreage. Nobody had yet petitioned the Department of the Interior for the right to bid on them. Were they only wasteland? Was Slick simply attempting to create a buyer's market before selling worthless sites at a profit? Sinclair thought not. He remembered Slick, who had at one time tried to sell him some leases, as a cadaverous fellow with burning eyes and a mop of white hair; he remembered, too, the intensity with which the man had sworn to him that he would become a millionaire. And there was something else to consider. The country around Slick's well was dotted with blackjack oaks. Sinclair believed in drilling close to blackjacks—and in graveyards, for that matter. He started purchasing the unclaimed Creek land, and soon the Cushing Field, the site of half a dozen boomtowns, returned him fortunes from its 455 million barrels of petroleum.

Sinclair later brought adversity upon himself by bribing the Secretary of the Interior, Albert B. Fall, during the Teapot Dome scandal; he spent seven and a half months in a federal prison and was forced to give $12,156,246 to the United States Treasury for petroleum that he had illegally extracted from naval reserves in Wyoming. However, by then he was so wealthy that his enormous oil empire was not seriously affected by this setback.

The rich and powerful promoters like Sinclair risked a considerable amount of the capital that helped support the great boom in the Southwest. However, its flavor was compounded by the hordes of smaller fry—drillers, leasers, tool dressers, roustabouts and teamsters who hurried from one strike to the next—and by the brigades of prostitutes, shysters, saloonkeepers, cardsharps and thieves who battened on them in the noisy, muddy, smoke-hung towns in which they gambled, fought and spent their pay.

Oil-field hands were a rough lot—clannish, proud of their dangerous trades, long-suffering and as scornful of those who were content with softer lives as were the backwoodsmen and keelboaters of an earlier West. One roustabout reflected the attitudes and preoccupations of many another toiler in the roaring Cushing Field when he scribbled the following schedule on the back of an envelope that was preserved, by chance, for posterity:

11:00 A.M.—Get up
11:00-11:30—Sober up
11:30-noon—Eat
Noon to midnight—Work like hell
Midnight to 3:00 A.M.—Get drunk
3:00-3:30—Beat hell out of them that's got it coming
3:30—Go to bed

Each raw new town was washed into being, like flotsam piling up in a flood, by the torrents of money that spilled into the Southwest after every strike. Six

hundred thousand dollars was spent every 24 hours for drilling in the Ranger Field in Texas during 1919, while more than half a million was flowing into leases and a quarter of a million a day was paid for petroleum coming out of the ground. A million dollars a week was expended on construction in the towns of Ranger and Eastland alone and uncounted millions more went into expanding tank-car yards and building five new railroads into the oil fields of the area. This maelstrom of cash drew opportunists of every stripe into widening acres of shacks and tents: 30,000 came to Ranger,

Stock dealers—many with nicknames like "Block Five" and "Over the Top"—sell Texas oil shares on a Wichita Falls sidewalk in 1919. Although much of the boom stock was of no value, an occasional lucky investor doubled his investment.

This 1929 stock certificate, unlike shares of many fly-by-night Southwest outfits, was well worth the paper it was printed on. The 10-year-old Texon Company, originally capitalized at two million dollars, was worth some $19 million by then.

10,000 to Eastland, 10,000 to Breckenridge and 16,000 to Desdemona, while thousands more were clotting up in the peripheral towns of Cisco, DeLeon, Comanche, Gorman, Caddo, Necessity, Frankell, Edhobby and Gunsight.

Saloons, dance halls and whorehouses materialized as if by magic in every oil town, but beds, food, water and most other ordinary amenities of life became scarce as the boomers and their parasites came hurrying in. Laundries were practically nonexistent: most oilfield hands threw their clothes away every few weeks and purchased new outfits. A bath could cost a dollar when and if the boomer could find a rentable bathtub and a glass of water was as much as 50 cents at restaurants—most of which employed gun-toting toughs to maintain order, meter the flow of customers and throw out those who were foolish enough to complain about the quality of the food that was served. Grocery stores in Caddo had bread and other staples delivered from Fort Worth by parcel post as the cheapest means of transportation, even though the overworked post offices were piled high with unsorted mail.

The pleasures and perils of striking it rich

Forced out of Kansas in the 1870s and relocated on scrubby, unproductive land in northeastern Oklahoma, the Osage Indians seemed destined to lead lives of grinding poverty, forever dependent on government handouts. About the only thing to be said for their rolling, barren property was that nobody wanted it.

But the discovery of oil changed all that. White men took a sudden, fiercely competitive interest in Osage land, and by the '20s, oil leases, auctioned under an elm in Pawhuska, Oklahoma, were bringing dizzying prices. The Indians made millions and some companies that bought leases, including Phillips and Sinclair, became major oil producers. Understandably, the tribe and oilmen were very cordial with one another.

The Osage became the richest Indian tribe, if not the richest ethnic group, per capita, in the world. An average family of five had an income of $65,000 a year, a fortune in that era. The Osage became conspicuous consumers, with luxury cars and fancy clothes leading their shopping lists. They were famous for buying new Cadillacs or Pierce Arrows, driving them until they broke down and ditching them beside the road.

But if their black gold bought luxury, it also bought sorrow and death. There were almost as many schemes to separate the Osage from their money as there were Indians. Swindle and murder became frighteningly common. Chief Fred Lookout said in the '30s that someday the oil would be gone, and with it regular checks, fine cars and new clothes. "Then," he said, "I know my people will be happier." His prophecy was never tested: money kept rolling in, and the Osage were never able to escape it.

Frank Phillips, founder of Phillips Petroleum, wears a chief's headdress among Osage Indians who honored him in 1930 for paying record sums for oil leases.

A "shooter" prepares nitroglycerin to be exploded in a well to start oil flow. Some blasts were premature. "Mr. Wright's hands," a newspaper wrote of one shooter, "were found yards from the scene."

Workers at a Wyoming oil field tighten a set of valves to control a spouting well. Capping a gusher was sometimes as difficult as finding oil in the first place—and more dangerous, because of the risk of fire.

the hole at the end of a cable, and fired them by dropping an explosive device known as a go-devil—usually a time bomb—after them. Wells that were emitting gas, however, had a way of regurgitating the shell before it reached bottom, and of killing the shooter who was not fast enough to escape before it reappeared "like a feather floating over a hot radiator" and blew up derrick, boiler, machinery and everything else in the vicinity. But there were shooters who stood their ground in the face of such horrifying dilemmas and lived to tell the tale.

A driller named Walter Cline recalled how one shooter, Tom Mendenhall, dealt with the problem. "When we let the second bucket down, the gas just caught it and began to push it back up. Well, the only thing I could think of was running for the tall uncut timber. Tom was standing right by the well. And he put his head down and he could hear the glycerin bucket scraping on the side of the casing as it came up, and he said, 'Don't run off, Walter. I'll take care of it.'

And so foolish me, I stood there to see what he was going to do, and he did something I wouldn't do at all. He just spread his legs on each side of the casing and waited until the gas pushed this bucket of liquid nitroglycerin right up. And when it got up about waist high, he just reached out and hugged it like he was coming home to mamma, and picked it up the rest of the way and took it over to the corner of the derrick and set it down."

No shooter became quite so famous for derring-do as W. A. ("Tex") Thornton, a Mississippi physician's son who carried a container of nitroglycerin into the heart of a well fire at Electra, Texas, in 1919, and blew out the flames after retreating to a safe distance. Thornton protected himself with a makeshift covering made of asbestos and later ordered an asbestos suit from the Johns-Manville Company—a get-up that earned him the sobriquet of "the human salamander." Steam had been used, up to this time, as an extinguishing agent for burning oil or gas wells, a dubious process that

A dense cloud of black smoke from burning oil tanks churns into the sky at Drumright, Oklahoma, in 1914. Conflagrations like this one were so commonplace in the boomtime Southwest that local citizens calmly went about their business while entire oil fields were in flames.

The boomtime prestige of Texas oilmen put Jesse C. McDowell, a Beaumont, Texas, petroleum executive, on the cover of the April 1902 issue of *Successful American,* a New York magazine. Inside the magazine, all four of the feature articles dealt with prominent Texans.

end of the big, fast money that had fueled the boom.

Joiner, now remembered as the King of the Wildcatters, was a rare old bird, indeed—as famous in the oil fields for his addiction to book reading and his penchant for quoting from Shakespeare and the Bible as for his endless bad luck. He had begun seeking petroleum late in life, having been a storekeeper in Alabama and a self-educated lawyer and legislator in Tennessee before wandering to Oklahoma in 1897. He had been the first to drill over two great reservoirs of petroleum in Oklahoma—the Seminole Field and the Cement Pool in Caddo County—but had run out of money before tapping either. Few wildcatters drilled as doggedly with ramshackle equipment or coped with disappointment more philosophically than he.

Joiner was 65 years old and possessed little more than a suitcase full of dirty shirts when he arrived in Dallas in 1925 and started scrounging money for a new try amid cut-over pinelands and scrubby cotton farms west of the Sabine River in East Texas. Geologists were certain that his chosen basin was a hopeless location because it did not have salt domes, but Joiner persisted and managed to lease about 10,000 acres after two years of short rations and fast talk. He erected a wooden derrick in August 1927, installed two worn-out boilers he called Big Joe and Little Joe, and began drilling on a farm that was owned by a widow named Daisy Bradford.

There were those who said that old Dad was less interested in wildcatting in his declining years than in using his decrepit rig as an excuse to raise enough money to keep eating. He had chosen his site simply because Mrs. Bradford had refused to lease her 975 acres to him until he promised to look for oil there first, and he spent more time selling stock in his venture to local farmers, thereafter, than in actual drilling. His bit got stuck when Daisy Bradford No. 1 was 1,098 feet deep and he needed funds before he could skid his rig downhill to start again 100 feet away. Daisy Bradford No. 2 became inoperable at 2,518 feet and he was therefore forced to move his equipment once more, having accomplished absolutely nothing in two long years of endeavor.

Daisy Bradford No. 3 went down only sporadically; Joiner's crew, during the periods when he could keep one intact, spent much of their time cutting wood for the boilers and making repairs. It took seven months to reach 1,500 feet. But Joiner, a spry, amiable and ingratiating old codger, had come to represent hope to Rusk County's impoverished farmers: here was a man who might make them all rich. They took his stock certificates in return for labor and supplies and used scrip that he issued in exchange for groceries as a substitute for currency. Farmers toiled for him as roustabouts. A banker's wife from nearby Overton cooked for the old man and the crew.

Nonetheless, Joiner seemed to be as surprised as everyone else when Daisy Bradford No. 3—which was down to 3,592 feet after 17 months of drilling—started gurgling audibly in October 1930. He was even more startled when it started spraying oil over a crowd of 5,000 creditors, leaseholders and stockholders who had gathered around as if by magic upon hearing of big doings at the well. "I dreamed it would happen," Joiner commented, "but I never really believed it."

His dream expanded during the next few months. He had tapped what geologists refer to as the Woodbine Sand—which was the subterranean residue of a prehistoric sea—and had discovered a pool that later proved to contain six billion barrels of oil. Daisy Bradford No. 3 brought Dad Joiner the first real money of his life—$1.2 million pressed upon him by a former gambler named H. L. Hunt, who then made $100 million in return and went on to become one of the richest men in the United States.

Joiner's strike inspired the most reckless of the oil rushes—and the one that finally ended the boomtown ethos of the West. A thousand wells began leeching the East Texas field in the eight months following his triumph with Daisy Bradford No. 3. The price of oil plummeted from $1.30 a barrel in 1930 to five cents a barrel by 1931. The waste was appalling: for every barrel of oil that was shipped from the field, 10 more oozed back into the subsoil. Government researchers warned those who would listen that the United States was "exhausting its petroleum reserves at a dangerous rate."

The state of Texas imposed limits on production—in part to head off similar restrictions by the federal government—and did so in spite of strong opposition from free-wheeling oilmen. Petroleum bootleggers installed secret refineries in response, and fed them by laying a maze of illegal pipes underneath East Texas and by siphoning "hot oil" from the 42-mile-long pool that Joiner had discovered. It was necessary to call out the Texas National Guard in order to make the new rules stick, but they did enforce compliance in the end.

Other states in the West joined Texas in controlling the production of oil. Small landowners abandoned their dreams of obtaining enormous wealth through wildcat strikes on the back forty, although many were able to achieve a steadier prosperity from the return on oil wells that were tapped for a few barrels a day or for a few full days a month. Wildcatters became choosier about picking drilling sites; the less adventurous of roustabouts drifted off to more prosaic employment; and many a prostitute and gambler was forced into honest toil as speculative capital dried up and the big boom died slowly away.

Dad Joiner's million dollars were swept away in a blizzard of lawsuits that were brought by 150 people who had invested in his shares and who were unsatisfied with their reward. Joiner took this final disappointment in good part. He retreated to Dallas, where he lived on donations from oilmen who were luckier than he, basked in his reputation as the greatest of wildcatters—and, as always, read. He achieved a quieter but no less satisfying sort of fame as a result: he held the all-time record for withdrawing books from the Dallas Public Library when he died at the age of 87 in 1947.

6 | The myth in motion

On July 3, 1901, near Wagner, Montana, a gang of armed men stopped a train, dynamited its express car and rode off with $40,000. The robbery was the final fling of Butch Cassidy's Wild Bunch, whose exploits had been widely celebrated in newspapers and pulp magazines. But just as spreading civilization was curbing the activities of such brazen Western outlaws, a new and powerful medium was about to dramatize them as never before.

Two years after the Wild Bunch's last holdup, inventor Thomas A. Edison's New York film company showed a nine-minute Western film called *The Great Train Robbery*. It was a sensation; audiences saw, in motion, depictions of the deeds they had read about, and they happily ignored such incongruities as the Eastern locations.

Earlier films had given briefer glimpses of stereotyped Western characters even before the turn of the century. But *The Great Train Robbery* was a full-fledged Western; it told a tale of crime, pursuit and showdown that touched the core of the Western myth and brought it to life with outdoor action as only a movie could.

Subsequent early Westerns did little to develop the movies' potential for movement and spectacle. But once the industry moved to California after 1910, cameras recorded real Western scenery, and some film makers created vivid pictures of a way of life that had faded only a few years before—pictures that have done more than any books of history or fiction to shape the nation's image of the Old West.

A cinematographer stands at his hand-cranked camera as the director instructs the cast of a frontier drama at the Edison Company's Bronx studios in 1910. Mercury vapor lamps provide lighting.

192

Wild West types assemble behind a jug of "red eye" for a static saloon tableau called *Cripple Creek Barroom*. The earliest known Western, the film was made in 1898 and lasted less than a minute. In such primitive films, characters like the barmaid at right were often played by men.

195

The villains scuttle off with the loot in *The Great Train Robbery*, 1903, the first Western movie to tell a story, and the one that set the pattern for later Westerns. The film included such classic elements as a horseback chase and a saloon scene with bullies forcing a dude to dance.

Miners scurry to file their claims in *A Race for Millions*, a 1906 short climaxed by a main-street shoot-out. As the horse opera came of age, painted backdrops like these gave way to outdoor sets and later to vistas of the real West.

The great roundup at Hollywood and Vine

One must doubt that the theater, for all its antiquity, ever attracted acolytes less enamored of grease paint than the cowhands who drifted into Hollywood after 1910 to become mounted extras in early Western movies. The town's odd new industry made stars of a few of them, but these men had not come to California to be actors and they were often secretly contemptuous of the lesser mortals who had. The cowhands, refugees from declining ranches, rodeos and Wild West shows, had heard that the studios would pay a man five dollars a day plus a box lunch for riding and roping, and had headed for the Coast simply to avoid the ignominy of employment afoot.

They looked upon Hollywood as a kind of last trail town and treated it as such even after streetcars arrived from Los Angeles and palm trees were planted along the boulevards. They created a closed society of their own in which a man was judged by the way he rode a horse, used his fists and held his liquor; they drank and played poker at a café called The Waterhole, where tequila and mescal were served in coffee cups through the long years of Prohibition; they bought fancy footgear from a Mexican bootmaker named Joe Posada, creased their Stetsons according to strict convention to show to the initiated what part of cattle country they hailed from, and generally did what they could to make themselves at home off the range as they grew used to the curious, often bone-shattering tasks demanded by new bosses who bawled at them through megaphones.

Employment was uncertain since it was mostly obtained by hanging around The Waterhole or a horse barn on Sunset Boulevard until some studio sent an automobile to pick up riders, or by sitting in a wire cage at Universal's San Fernando Valley lot to await the needs of directors who were filming Westerns. Still, the pay was better than any of them had ever earned punching cattle—movie people paid them a lot more for falling off broncs, they said sardonically, than they had ever been paid for staying on them—and a man with a reputation for skill and daring was given ample opportunity to demonstrate its validity to a community of his peers. Six-horse teams were fully as difficult to control from the seat of a plunging stagecoach on a Hollywood back lot as they had ever been on roads out of Deadwood or Cheyenne, and the stunts that were incorporated increasingly into shoot-'em-ups after 1920 demanded a rare combination of recklessness and precision from the men who performed them.

The simplest and most common stunt involved the use of a notorious device known as the Running W—a pair of wires attached to hobbles on a horse's front fetlocks and connected to a ring that the rider held in one hand after mounting. Men destined to bite the dust while tearing along at a gallop simply kicked their feet free of their stirrups, aimed one shoulder at the ground, tripped the horse by yanking the wires and hoped they would not break any bones as the unfortunate beast went down.

A variation of this bit of stagecraft, the Stationary W or Dead Man Fall, was more dangerous yet: the tripping device was anchored to a buried post by 80 or 100 yards of piano wire and the rider was catapulted out of the saddle without warning as the horse was slammed to earth at the end of its invisible tether.

The men who took these risks lived by their own hard code and judged others by it too, however exalted their positions in the Hollywood hierarchy. They expected directors or stars, especially those who had risen

Screen cowboy William S. Hart's flinty gaze, seen in a still from an early film, reinforced the sharp realism of his films. "The truth of the West," he wrote in 1929, "meant more to me than a job."

from the ranks, to behave with a cowhand's lack of pretense, and spoke of them with mingled pity and scorn—for all their big cars, big houses and expensive blondes—if they did not.

They considered William S. Hart a ham as well as an Easterner, though he had spent his boyhood in the West and honored its traditions as much as any of them; they accused Cecil B. De Mille of demanding riding scenes likely to result in unscripted accidents—thus achieving pileups awful enough to satisfy his sense of theater without paying the extra wages awarded for planned stunts. They liked the young director, John Ford—a New England Irishman—for his bluff, convivial manner and obvious talent. But two roughnecks named Hoot Gibson and Art Acord were the sort of Hollywood celebrities they could take unreservedly to heart.

Edmund Richard (Hoot) Gibson was one of the most successful and enduring of Western heroes; he possessed something of Will Rogers' rustic humor and made millions—all eventually lost—starring in scores of low-budget horse operas in the 1920s, '30s and early 1940s. Artemus Ward Acord had none of Gibson's on-screen humor; his career was rooted in his extraordinary physical abilities. He was a violent, mercurial man who fell prey to liquor and drugs and vanished into Mexico, where he died in 1931, stabbed to death, according to one story, by a jealous husband.

Both men were Westerners, Gibson having grown up in Nebraska and Acord in Oklahoma. Both had punched cattle, both had worked in Wild West shows, and both had broken into pictures as extras and stunt men. They were consummate riders. Gibson had been judged best all-around cowboy at the Pendleton Round-Up in 1912 and Acord, who bested Gibson for a similar title in 1916, was, in the minds of many cowboys who had seen him in action, the greatest of all Western horsemen. Their rodeo rivalry continued in Hollywood when they found themselves together on the Universal lot; they competed not as movie stars vying for big box office, but as two cowhands just off the range, each bent on proving himself the better man.

Gibson earned a reputation for recklessness from his early days as a stunt man. A director offered him five dollars, on one occasion, to let himself be dragged by a galloping horse. "Make it ten," said Hoot, "and I'll let

him kick me to death!" Acord was known to be even more willfully self-destructive; he was celebrated for sticking to a bucking bronco that carried him through a six-strand barbed-wire fence. The two actors achieved a mutual notoriety at Universal for the way they went after each other with their fists: Acord once marched onto a set where his colleague was working and shouted, "Gibson, I can whip your ass!" He took a wild swing and broke his hand on a stable post. Gibson bellowed, "Good . . . you son of a bitch!" and hammered his foe with unmerciful gusto.

But men like Gibson and Acord are remembered for more than recklessness and belligerence. They were central participants in the codification of the Western myth. Their flickering images gave permanent life to the myth's basic elements: the gunfight in the dusty street, the encircled wagon train, the holdup of the stagecoach, the confrontation in the frontier saloon, the defense of vulnerable womanhood (whether dance-hall

Hoot Gibson ropes a desperado in one of a spate of Westerns he made in the 1920s. The scripts did not vary, but he drew such crowds that in 1924 Universal guaranteed him a million dollars over three years.

Fists clenched tightly, Broncho Billy Anderson scowls over a foe in a barroom brawl in *The Golden Trail*. Anderson acted in some 375 Westerns while head of Essanay Studios from 1907 to 1917.

girl with heart of gold or blushing schoolma'am fresh from Philadelphia) and the clash of posse with rustlers, or of cavalry with whooping Apaches.

And no matter how far from historical truth Hollywood's mythmakers might wander in the service of entertainment, the demeanor of cowboy extras and the harshness of Western scenery gave their moving pictures a verisimilitude unapproached by literature or any kind of theater the world had seen before. Not only were Hollywood's sagas of the West played out against vistas of real mountains and real deserts, but they were peopled with scores of men who rode, dressed and bellied up to saloon bars as if they worked for the Aztec Land & Cattle Company itself, as, indeed, some of them had.

The men who made Westerns were engaged in entertainment for all that, since the movies were based on concepts of theater, rather than concepts of history—a curious kind of theater that had its beginnings in

penny arcades and nickelodeons in the East and that had been dominated from the start by entrepreneurs from the fur and garment businesses. (One of them, Universal Pictures' "Uncle Carl" Laemmle, once said to an actor's agent, "Act he can, maybe, but my God who made his buttonholes?") New York was the film capital of the United States in the early years after Thomas Alva Edison invented his kinetoscope peep show and then adapted it to project moving pictures on a screen. The celebrated early Western, *The Great Train Robbery,* a trailblazer in cinematic storytelling, was shot on a section of the Delaware and Lackawanna Railroad near Dover, New Jersey.

Before *The Great Train Robbery* appeared in 1903, kinetoscopes and primitive theaters had exhibited minute-long vignettes with titles like *Procession of Mounted Indians and Cowboys, Calf Branding, Buffalo Bill and Escort* and *Cripple Creek Barroom.* But *The Great Train Robbery* ran a full nine minutes, and

203

A legend who put his own legend on film

In 1913, two decades after the last Indian wars ended, survivors from both sides gathered at South Dakota's Pine Ridge Agency to reenact six of their engagements for a novice movie producer named Buffalo Bill Cody.

Deeply in debt, the old Wild West showman hoped film making would be his financial salvation. With typical bravura, he wrote a quasi-documentary epic that included important battles, like Wounded Knee, plus some of his own escapades in lesser clashes, like the Battle of Summit Springs.

The aspiring movie mogul soon discovered that filming legendary events could be as hectic as living through them. His 74-year-old guest star, the famed Indian-fighter General Nelson Miles, was as vain and temperamental as any Hollywood headliner. Miles demanded that all 11,000 troops he led during the Wounded Knee campaign be represented on film (to placate him Cody craftily marched 300 soldiers past an empty camera 40 times).

Miles also insisted that the Wounded Knee battle scene be shot precisely where it had occurred 23 years before—over the mass grave of Sioux killed in the conflict. Outraged Indian extras vowed to defend the sacred ground by replacing the blank cartridges in their guns with live ammunition. Cody dissuaded them, but his troubles were not over. During filming, Indian actors "died" histrionically enough, but then kept lifting their heads to look at the continuing action.

The Last Indian Battles, or From the Warpath to the Peace Pipe was released in 1914. Though popular, it did not make enough money to clear Cody's debts. He returned to the arena, deciding that a film was "harder to organize and run than three circuses."

In a publicity still for his film, the aging Cody gazes out over plains he scouted as a young man. The troopers lying on the ground are two of the 300 soldiers he borrowed from the Army to use as extras.

Cody guns down an Indian—portraying Cheyenne Chief Tall Bull—who is about to tomahawk a female captive. The real-life rescue during the Battle of Summit Springs 44 years earlier was less dramatic.

During the reenactment of the Battle of Wounded Knee, soldiers clash with Sioux warriors. Indians complained that it was an inaccurate depiction of the fight—in which outnumbered Sioux, including women and children, were massacred.

its director, an Edison engineer named Edwin S. Porter, gave it unprecedented suspense, in that time, by inventing methods of visual narration that quickly became part of the basic grammar of the movies. Porter did not use subtitles; he told his story by cutting from scene to scene in violation of strict chronology, with only the logic of the story to carry the audience along. The picture shifts from a railroad telegraph office, where bandits bind and gag the operator, to the approaching train and the holdup, back to the telegraph office as the operator is freed by his little daughter, then to a saloon with the operator arriving to summon some avenging cowboys, back to the train as the robbers make their escape, and on to a chase and gun battle by which justice triumphs in the end.

The Great Train Robbery cost $150 to produce and was an instant sensation, the more so because of the way audiences screamed and fainted during a close-up (which opened or closed the film as exhibitors chose) of a bandit firing his pistol directly at the camera. The picture inspired many imitations—*The Little Train Robbery, The Bold Bank Robbery, The Hold-up of the Rocky Mountain Express*—and a second *Great Train Robbery* in which the Lubin Company of Philadelphia copied the original, scene for scene, changing only minor details such as a calendar in the telegraph office as evidence of originality for copyright purposes. But successful as *The Great Train Robbery* and its imitators were, they still lacked a crucial element—the hero—that was to make the Western an instrument of mass entertainment for decades to come.

This ingredient was supplied by a sometime actor named Gilbert M. Anderson who had appeared, briefly, as an extra in Porter's film. Anderson—a former salesman who had changed his name from Max Aronson when he decided to go on the stage—was shrewd enough to recognize that Porter had missed a commercial opportunity, since no memorable character had emerged from the picture's anonymous cast to be exploited in later films. He took up directing himself and in 1908, having formed the Essanay Company with a Chicago film equipment distributor named George K. Spoor, he headed for California to make Westerns of his own. He ended up not only producing and directing but starring in his own films, since the West Coast

boasted few actors, and since even those few equated movies with side shows and flea circuses and refused to have any part of them.

Anderson had embarrassing memories of *The Great Train Robbery*—his rented horse having thrown him repeatedly as he tried to urge it into camera range—but he got used to horses in time, donned chaps, gunbelt and Stetson, took a Western story from *The Saturday Evening Post* and made a primitive, sentimental little picture called *Broncho Billy and the Baby*.

The public was delighted, and Anderson gave them a sequel a week—among them *Broncho Billy's Redemption, Broncho Billy's Bible, Broncho Billy's Oath* and *Broncho Billy's Last Spree*—for the next seven years. Broncho Billy Anderson was neither handsome nor capable of cowboy stunts, but he had a look of beefy muscularity and eventually learned to twirl a lariat and sit a horse as though he was not in imminent danger of falling off. His Essanay pictures were clumsy adaptions of pulp stories or dime novels, never ran for more than two reels (roughly half an hour), and cost $800, on the average, to produce. But they proved themselves a constantly salable staple at the box office, grossed up to $50,000 apiece, and made Broncho Billy the first of a long line of Western motion-picture stars.

Other companies were not slow to tap the wonderfully constant wells of revenue that Broncho Billy had revealed: horse operas proliferated as the rest of the motion-picture industry followed Essanay west to take root beneath the Southern California sun. Westerns got bigger budgets, longer running times (eventually up to seven or eight reels) and larger casts. Film makers like David Wark Griffith and Thomas H. Ince elevated technical standards, utilized realistic scenic locations and added excitement by employing daredevil riders who performed dangerous stunts during chases and battle scenes.

Griffith played a curious role in the enhancement of the Western; he made a great many of them between 1908 and 1913 and enjoyed staging the outdoor action that suited them so well. He produced several—among them *The Goddess of Sagebrush Gulch, The Last Drop of Water* and *Fighting Blood*—that were remarkable for their day, though they seem important, when viewed in retrospect, mainly as exercises by which he schooled himself for later spectacles like *The Birth of a Nation* and *Intolerance*. Griffith, who came to be known as "the father of film technique," did not invent the close-up, the long shot, crosscutting or the fade-out, as some of his admirers have claimed, but he used these devices more inventively than other early film makers and left a heritage of method that later directors—most notably John Ford—employed thereafter in dramatizing Western themes.

Thomas Ince had little of Griffith's creative genius, but by 1913 he had developed an organization that turned out a picture a week—mainly Westerns, both features and shorts—and was in many respects the model for big-studio operations of the future. Ince went to Los Angeles in 1911, sent by two ex-bookmakers, Adam Kessel Jr. and Charles O. Bauman, to manage a movie studio in which they had invested after the State of New York banned horse racing. The studio turned out to be an abandoned grocery store converted into a makeshift film-processing laboratory, with a backyard stage that boasted a single backdrop depicting birds in flight. Ince was undeterred, not only because he had wrung a salary of $150 a week out of Bauman, but because he felt himself on the brink of opportunity. The pugnacious-looking, curly-haired, moon-faced young man was endowed with audacity and persuasiveness as well as a manic energy—which he attributed to the fact that his heart beat at an abnormally high rate—and soon talked the New York partners into an enlargement of operations that was to give Westerns new scope.

He discovered the Miller Brothers 101 Ranch Wild West show at winter quarters near Los Angeles and rented the whole operation for $2,500 a week, thereby equipping himself with cowboys, Indians, cattle, stagecoaches, horses and buffalo. He then bought 14,000 acres of sere landscape in the hills north of Santa Monica on which to deploy his new properties and set about simulating frontier conflict on a scale no previous Westerns had attempted. *War on the Plains, Battle of the Red Men, The Indian Massacre* and *The Lieutenant's Last Fight,* all filmed at "Inceville" in 1912, earned him recognition almost overnight as one of the industry's top film makers. These accomplishments were overshadowed, however—in their impact on the viewing public, and in the development of the Western itself—by his casual decision to let a middle-aged actor named William Surrey Hart experiment at playing a reformed outlaw in two pictures, and to give him his head thereafter.

Hart, an Easterner who had played Shakespeare, came to Western movies with a genuine sense of mission. He had seen a number of Western shorts and was outraged at the historical license their fantasies had taken with America's frontier tradition. He was determined to deliver the Western from such heresies and to use it to reflect something of the lives and values of the people who had actually settled the West. The movies' view of Western legend was subject to a kind of prismatic splitting, in consequence, after Hart made his debut at Inceville. The cheerfully unrealistic cowboy film persisted, and became a kind of incubator for the absurdities later visited upon the genre by Gene Autry, Roy Rogers and other singing cowboys. But Hart established a tradition of gritty authenticity that would be reflected in "epics" like *The Covered Wagon* and *The Iron Horse* and later big-budget Westerns.

Hart's righteousness about the Western was not as improbable as his Shakespearean background suggests. He was indeed from the East, born in Newburgh, New York, in 1870, but his father, a miller who had immigrated from Liverpool, soon headed west to build grain mills in Kansas, Minnesota and Dakota Territory. The boy saw great herds of Texas cattle being driven to railheads and learned to speak the Sioux language while playing with Indian children on the waning frontier. He adapted himself to life in New York City when the family moved east again in the middle 1880s, but still thought of himself as a "white Indian boy."

He studied acting briefly in England after working his way across the Atlantic and, on returning to the United States, he barnstormed the country playing Shakespeare and tawdry melodrama with down-at-the-heels theatrical troupes. He became celebrated eventually as an interpreter of Western roles and had starred in a succession of plays, including *The Squaw Man, The Virginian* and *The Trail of the Lonesome Pine,* by the time he saw his first Western movie and became obsessed with creating motion pictures of his own.

Ince was less than enthusiastic when Hart arrived in Los Angeles to present him with this idea in 1913. He was not convinced, in spite of his own success, that

Westerns had any commercial future, and he certainly did not see Hart, by now 43 years old, as the star who would keep customers flocking to the box office.

But Ince was riding high and could afford to take a risk on Hart, whom he had known in New York. The producer let Hart play the villain in two shorts and, with these completed, allowed him to help write his own leading role in two feature films: *The Bargain* and *On The Night Stage*. Hart left for New York thereafter, apparently feeling that he had done his bit to rescue Hollywood from itself. Ince soon discovered, however, that *The Bargain* was becoming a smash hit; he located Hart and offered him a contract at the cautious figure of $125 a week. Hart accepted in ignorance of the picture's success and later grew bitter at being forced to work for such a modest wage. But he did persuade Ince to give him full control of every picture he made, and eventually escaped the contract; his unique approach to Westerns proved so popular that when he died in 1946 he left an estate of one million dollars.

Hart was a tall, lean man with high cheekbones and piercing eyes; he seemed younger than he was, and the gauntness of his features—which he heightened, said irreverent extras, by sucking on an alum stick—gave him the menacing look of a dime-novel gunslinger. But he dressed himself and his fellow players in exactly the sort of worn clothing he remembered from Kansas in the days of the cattle drives, and his sets had the look of the shabby settlements that still existed in many parts of the West. His "ramshackle Western towns and their inhabitants" seemed sprung, in the words of film historian William K. Everson, from "unretouched Mathew Brady photographs" and gave the viewer "an ever-present sense of dry heat. (Panchromatic film stock, developed in the '20s, softened and glamorized the landscapes in later Westerns.)" His audiences saw clouds of dust, so omnipresent on the real frontier. "This naturalistic quality vanished later," Everson pointed out, "when directors took to wetting down the ground so that riding scenes would be cleaner and crisper."

But if Hart's films succeeded in creating the look of the Old West as he had known it, their stories were embellished with melodrama such as no cattle town had ever experienced. He began by casting himself as a

Tricks to enhance the West's flickering image

Paying visitors observe the filming of the

If an actor in an early Western movie mounted his horse lethargically, the cameraman just slowed up his machine and presto—when the film was projected at normal speed, the cowboy appeared to leap nimbly into the saddle. This technique was one of many used to enhance—or distort—reality in the version of the West that early film makers delivered to audiences.

Artificial lighting was expensive, so interior scenes were often filmed outdoors on sunlit sets like the open-top barroom below. And a few rows of false building fronts on studio back lots served as frontier towns in film after film, until those façades became warmly familiar to devoted movie fans.

Some film makers devised ingenious ways to overcome the problems of

shooting in majestic natural settings to give audiences a vision of the real West. But profit-minded Hollywood allowed little time for such artistic pursuits. If a crew arrived at the wrong location, the story would be altered and the scene shot anyway. "If the sun was shining, we were supposed to be turning out films," said director King Vidor. "And we usually did just that."

1916 Western *Love's Lariat* at Universal's California studio. The star of the film, Harry Carey, is holding both the girl and the gun.

In the 1920s a director uses an automobile as a moving camera platform for a head-on view of a following horseman and wagons.

To get just the angle he wants for a scene in *The Sky Pilot*, King Vidor directs Colleen Moore from a mid-river perch in 1921.

Stunt man Yakima Canutt does a second-story backdive into an off-camera fireman's net in Republic's all-purpose Western town.

"good bad man" who was moved to redemption by the love of a virtuous woman and, whether out of sentiment or shrewd business sense, he stuck to this formula—similar to one Broncho Billy had employed with success—in practically all the pictures he made.

Hart's notions of the West and his contributions to its mythology can be gleaned in part from the subtitles of one of his best films, *Hell's Hinges,* made in 1916. It opens in the East, where a young minister, described in a subtitle as *A weak and selfish youth, utterly unfit for the calling,* is being sent west by superiors bent on extricating him from the temptations of a big city. A stagecoach delivers him and his sister, Faith, to: *The town known on the government surveyor's maps as Placer Centre, but throughout the sun-baked territory as just plain "Hell's Hinges," and a good place to "ride wide of" . . . a gun-fighting, man-killing, devil's den of iniquity that scorched even the sun-parched soil on which it stood.*

The respectable folks in Placer Centre who stand ready to welcome the newcomer are but *a scant handful . . . a drop of water in a barrel of rum.* They are subject to the wiles of a villain, *Silk Miller: mingling the oily craftiness of a Mexican with the deadly treachery of a rattler, no man's open enemy, and no man's friend.*

Miller has given the job of running the new arrival out of town to Hart, who is introduced as: *Blaze Tracey, the embodiment of the best and worst of the early West. A man-killer whose philosophy of life is summed up in the creed: shoot first and do your disputin' afterwards.*

But Tracey has never seen a woman like Faith, who turns upon him *a different kind of smile, sweet, honest and trustful, and seeming to say, "How do you do, friend?"* A close-up shows Hart in the grip of doubt and even a sort of remorse: *One who is Evil, looking for the first time on that which is Good.*

Tracey takes no action against Faith's brother, but neither does he interfere with a mob that hoots and mocks the young preacher. He is moved to action, however, on Sunday. He enters a barn in which a service has been scheduled, finds the minister utterly cowed by a lawless mob, but sees Faith like *the eternal flame that shone over the blood-drenched roman arena* singing a hymn while drunken cowboys curse and

fire pistols in the air. He draws his own guns, crouches and intones: *I'm announcin' here and now that there ain't goin' to be no more pickin' on the parson's herd so long as they mind their own business.*

And to Faith, after quiet is restored: *I reckon God ain't wantin' me much, Ma'am, but when I look at you I feel I've been ridin' the wrong trail.*

(Convulsive piano music down front.)

The hero having cast his lot on the side of virtue, the pace of the action picks up. The villain directs his mistress, Dolly, to seduce the parson after plying him with drink, and tries to win Tracey back to his side by leading him to the saloon where the pair lie in a stupor on Dolly's bed. But Blaze is true to Faith and rides off to seek medical help for the parson. A saloon mob carries the drunken minister to the church, a fight takes place, the minister is killed, and the church goes up in flames.

Retribution, however, is at hand. Tracey returns at a gallop. He discovers Faith bending over the body of her brother, advances on the saloon, kicks open its doors, and shouts over drawn guns: *Hell needs this town, and it's goin' back, and goin' damn quick!*

He guns down the villain and holds his henchmen at bay (while gallantly allowing the dance-hall girls to escape) until he has ignited the wooden saloon by shooting out its kerosene lamps. The fire spreads and the whole town goes up in flames.

And then from the mothering sky came the baby dawn, singing as it wreathed the gray horns of the mountains with ribbons of rose and gold. Blaze finds Faith weeping upon her brother's grave; she rises and they walk, side by side, toward peaks now bathed in the fresh sunlight of a new day.

Whatever the future, theirs to share together. . . .

Hart's motion pictures, with their curious blend of sentimentality and realism, were enormously popular for almost 10 years and helped to shape the myth of the West for millions as movies became the dominant entertainment medium. However, by the mid-1920s, Hart was getting too old to play young romantic leads, and the public had become tired of his rigid formula. His final and most ambitious effort, *Tumbleweeds*—a drama of the Cherokee Strip land rush, filmed in 1925 at a cost of $312,000—was one of the first Western epics, but it failed at the box office.

DAMSELS NOT ALWAYS IN DISTRESS

Unlike the consistent cowboy hero — who was almost always tough, resolute and supremely masculine — the female lead in Western movies was presented in a variety of character patterns that differed according to the plot and when the film was made. Originally, and throughout most of the 1920s, she was often portrayed as the strong pioneer heroine *(below, left)*, fully capable of defending herself. Later, she was softened into the stereotype of the frail, helpless woman, forever turning to her hero for protection *(right)*. Toward the end of the 1930s, she again emerged as a demonstrably self-reliant and increasingly robust figure *(below, right)* — this time with overt sex appeal.

Gary Cooper offers a consoling shoulder to a frightened Mary Brian in 1929's *The Virginian*.

Anita Stewart is the independent woman in the 1920 movie, *The Fighting Shepherdess*.

Jimmy Stewart fends off Marlene Dietrich in the 1939 Western, *Destry Rides Again*.

Tom Mix tests his lasso in this 1926 publicity photograph for *The Canyon of Light*. Mix's immaculate costumes and daring stunts entranced audiences, making him the most popular silent-era cowboy.

In *My Pal the King*, Tom Mix is joined by child star Mickey Rooney as a European boy monarch. Mix cared little about the West and transported his cowboy hero as far away as Arabia, India and Manhattan.

Thomas Edwin (Tom) Mix had long since taken over as the movies' preeminent cowboy star by selling flamboyant showmanship rather than Hart's dusty authenticity laced with melodrama. Mix inspired scores of white-hatted cowboy heroes and a thousand formula B-Westerns, and kept himself in the public eye for years after Hart was all but forgotten.

Mix, like Hart, billed his horse as costar. But while Hart retired his mount, Fritz, early in his career (to spite Ince after a quarrel over finances), Mix's trick horse, Tony, became the best known animal in show business until Rin-Tin-Tin appeared. Again like Hart, Mix directed his own early pictures. But Mix was unhampered by any passion for realism and indulged an appetite for outrageous stunts that made his movies far less predictable than those of his fading rival. Mix came equipped, in fact, with a talent for embroidering the

truth; he not only billed himself as America's Champion Cowboy, but invented a collection of biographical data, accepted by many an interviewer, that should have tried the credulity of a child of five.

There were a good many versions of this life story, but Mix claimed, at one time or another, to have been born in a log cabin near El Paso, Texas (to a father who had served as an officer with the Seventh U.S. Cavalry and a mother with Cherokee blood), and to have attended the Virginia Military Institute before (1) joining the Texas Rangers, (2) serving as a scout and courier for a General Chafee (and being wounded in action) during the Spanish-American War, (3) taking part in both the Boxer Rebellion and the Philippine Insurrection and (4) going to Africa to break horses for the British Army during the Boer War. Mix also recalled acting as a wilderness guide for Theodore Roo-

sevelt, doing a term as sheriff of Two Buttes County, Colorado, serving as a U.S. marshal in Montana and New Mexico, capturing the "nefarious" Shonts brothers, fighting (and barely escaping a firing squad) in the Mexican Revolution and excelling in rodeos before accepting fame and fortune in Hollywood.

Mix was a good athlete; he rode well enough to do his own stunts, having learned to handle horses as a boy from his teamster father. He had also been both a soldier and a performer in Wild West shows. But he had been born and raised in Pennsylvania, not Texas, he had never attended VMI, and there is no evidence that he saw any action at all after joining the Army at the outbreak of the Spanish-American War. Most of the excitement he experienced in youth seems to have stemmed from his life-long propensity for getting married. He deserted the Army and headed for Oklahoma City and a job tending bar at the behest of his first wife, Grace Allen, whom he met in Virginia. He

hooked up with the saloonkeeper's daughter, Kitty Jewel Perrine, after Grace left him, and when Kitty Jewel walked out on him as well, he married a Montana ranch girl, Olive Stokes.

Mix seemed unable to resist women who caught his fancy. He was to spend fortunes, after parting with Olive, on two more wives—actress Victoria Forde and trapeze performer Mabel Hubbell Ward. But women were always secondary to his dream—nurtured since he had seen a Wild West show as a boy of 10—of becoming a latter-day Buffalo Bill. He managed to ingratiate himself with the famed Miller brothers after settling in Dewey, Oklahoma, and wangled a job as a rider with their 101 Ranch Wild West show.

He was working as a deputy marshal in Dewey in 1909 when a crew from the Selig Polyscope Company came to town to shoot a documentary on ranching. Mix hired on as a handler of livestock, appeared in a bronc-busting sequence and stayed with the crew as

they traveled about the West. He starred in a couple of
fictional Western shorts and later went to California
with another Selig crew, which hoped to capture some
of Broncho Billy's audience with crude one- and two-
reel Westerns. Mix made almost a hundred of these
nondescript little movies over the following eight
years and learned his trade so well—he was paid to
produce and direct as well as rope and ride—that
when an ex-nickelodeon operator named William Fox
hired him to make feature films in 1917 he became
an instant sensation.

Mix gave Westerns a fresh dimension: a hard-riding
hero who never, never drank, smoked, swore or suffered the indignity of uncombed hair. "I ride into a place
owning my own horse and saddle," he said in defining
his roles. "It isn't my quarrel, but I get into trouble
doing the right thing for somebody else. I never get any
money reward. I may be made foreman of the ranch and
I get the girl, but there is never a fervid love scene." He
pulled his guns only in extreme circumstances and almost never killed villains when forced to draw; he
preferred to overcome them in fistfights staged atop
freight cars or on the edges of cliffs or, better yet, by
lassoing them and tying them up.

He took to wearing white ten-gallon hats, gloves
and costumes that seemed to have been designed as
loungewear for a Mexican general. His stunts involved
airplanes, locomotives, cars and other impedimenta
never encountered by riders on the Chisholm Trail.

Mix was earning $17,500 a week by 1925 (his
pictures provided the Fox Film Corporation with the
lion's share of its income) and attracting as much attention by his gaudy style of living as by his performances
on the screen. He built himself a Hollywood mansion
and equipped it with an English butler and a huge
electric sign on the lawn that displayed his initials in
lights at night. He collected a succession of silver-
trimmed, custom-built automobiles and a quarter-
million dollars worth of Western artifacts (put on display, after his death, at the Tom Mix Museum in
Dewey, Oklahoma). He made headlines with public
appearances, most notably when he took Tony (the
only horse ever ridden up a flight of stairs at the Paris
opera) on a tour of European cities. He made his last
movie in 1935 but was still a star to millions in the
autumn of 1940 when he took a curve too fast in

one of his fancy cars and died of a broken neck near
Florence, Arizona.

Mix turned the simple cowboy into a hero who
loomed larger than life for generations of youngsters,
not only because he appeared in more than 300 motion
pictures of his own, but because his costumes, stunts
and showman's approach to the Westerns were so
successful as to engender three decades of imitative
effort by other film makers. Once the horse opera had
been proven so elastic a form of entertainment, there
was hardly an actor from Nelson Eddy to Boris Karloff
who did not appear in at least one Western of some
description. And there were few movie studios that did
not crank out B-Westerns as staple products in order to
provide themselves with cash for more ambitious and
riskier ventures.

Yet for all the profits they made from cheap horse
operas, studios were only now and then willing to risk
big budgets or big stars on first-class Westerns. With a
few worthy exceptions, Westerns of the 1920s and
'30s were disdained as potboilers for the Saturday
matinee audience, and were left in the hands of Mix and
his imitators while top stars made more prestigious
pictures at the other end of the lot.

Only one major star of this period could move freely
between Westerns and more adult fare—a tall Montanan named Frank J. (Gary) Cooper. He was Paramount's top male box-office attraction and was not
squandered on assembly-line oaters, but appeared in far
more Westerns, nevertheless, than other actors of com-
parable stature. Cooper was eminently likable when
playing a foreign legionnaire, a flying ace, a doughboy
or an artist, but his lanky grace and understated virility
gave him instant authority when he was called back to
the saddle again.

He was born and grew up in Montana and worked
as a ranch hand before drifting into films—at the suggestion of some range friends he met during a visit to
Los Angeles—as an extra and stunt man in 1925. But
Cooper was no ordinary Hollywood cowboy. His father was a British-trained barrister and gentleman-
rancher who served as a justice of the Montana Supreme Court; young Cooper had attended an English
public school before college and had planned on a career as a cartoonist before being diverted by the fortunes that were the reward of motion-picture success.

Good Indians and bad Indians, but rarely a real Indian

In 1941 Juan Concha, leader of some Taos Indians performing in a film called *Valley of the Sun,* asked his tribesmen to work overtime to finish up a scene. Replied one: "Nope, we tired playing Indian. Go home."

As his comment indicates, Indians and their history were almost never portrayed on film with candor or realism. Though some of the silent films, including *The Squaw Man, The Invaders* and *The Vanishing American,* did recognize that Indians had received less than a fair shake from westward-bound whites, movies generally slid quickly over that distasteful theme into glib melodrama. Most of

the talkies portrayed Indians as nothing more than animated props—a dramatic part of a threatening landscape, perhaps, but no more individually delineated than lions in a safari movie.

Film makers very rarely bothered to research the realities of tribal existence. In one early silent, *The Mended Lute,* two forbidden Dakota lovers made good their escape in a canoe, a conveyance unknown to that buffalo-hunting Plains tribe. In *The Frontiersman,* a picture released by MGM in 1927, Southeastern Creek tribesmen were depicted as living in tipis, which they would not have had the hides to build even if they had preferred

them to their thatch lodges. At times unreality bordered on the absurd. In the 1920 version of *The Last of the Mohicans,* Wallace Beery, as Magua, stalked through the forest sporting rolled-down socks that showed above his moccasins.

The Indians that most American movie-goers came to know were all but mute primitives. Indians friendly to whites, like the Lone Ranger's faithful companion, Tonto (his name is the Spanish word for fool), communicated simple thoughts and cannily followed trails that seemed nearly invisible but never demonstrated more than a minimal amount of emotion or intelligence.

Dustin Farnum clutches his wife, Red Wing, as she dies in *The Squaw Man.* Seldom was there a happy ending for mixed-race couples.

Chief Thunder Cloud, who played Tonto, starred with Lee Powell in a *Lone Ranger* serial. The full-blooded Cherokee used a sun lamp to make his skin dark enough to make him a convincing screen Indian.

Richard Dix plays the classic noble savage cheated out of his tribal homelands in *The Vanishing American*. Noted an English critic: "It began finely. But how cheap and how trivial they made the story."

Ruthless warriors leave a party of white surveyors to die in *The Invaders*. Any sympathy audiences might have felt for Indian characters in early films was often dispelled by such grisly massacre scenes.

Cooper was given a featured part in *The Winning of Barbara Worth* after little more than a year as a mounted extra, and made such an impression on audiences that Paramount offered him a contract forthwith and was soon casting him as a leading man. He made his debut in sound pictures in the title role of *The Virginian,* from Owen Wister's novel. The book had been twice dramatized in silent movies but this third version—one of the first Western talkies—was such a success that it was re-released six years later by popular demand. Cooper's soft-spoken, honorable cowhand— his essential screen persona—made him, for millions, the definitive Westerner of film. He crossed and re-crossed the gulf between cowboy roles and more prestigious parts repeatedly thereafter.

But segregation was the rule for other actors: a straight dramatic or comedy star could essay only an occasional Western epic or spoof, while a Western star almost never appeared in anything but Westerns—in many cases because he was contracted to a "poverty row" company like Monogram or Resolute that made little else. The first crop of post-Mix heroes—Ken Maynard, Buck Jones, Tim McCoy, Fred Thomson, Bob Steele—worked year after year exclusively in Westerns without ever seeming to cherish ambitions toward "serious" acting or even greater stardom. Like Mix, they were fine athletes and usually did their own stunts; most of them had worked in rodeo or in Wild West shows. Later B-picture Western stars— Gene Autry, Roy Rogers, William Boyd—had to be taught to ride and used doubles, filmed at long range, for most of their stunts. However, audiences did not object: Autry's box-office success kept Republic Pictures solvent through the late 1930s, just as Mix had done for Fox in the 1920s.

Fans expected death-defying deeds from these latter-day cowboys and an ability to subdue the most malevolent of villains. They also came to assume, thanks to Mix, that Western heroes would obey codes of behavior that would have tried the resolution of a Trappist monk. Movie cowboys were bashful in the presence of women, young and old, and while they sometimes kissed the heroine, they usually had to be nudged into the clinch by their horses and seemed bent, after freeing themselves, on a shot of sarsaparilla or a glass of fresh buttermilk as an antidote for shaken nerves.

These curious conventions were unknown in the day of Harry Carey, William Farnum, Farnum's brother Dustin and other pioneers of Western silent films. But Hollywood demanded the strictures, once Mix had cleansed the cowboy of any hint of original sin and had made it pay at the box office. Studios seldom laid down rules of behavior as specific, however, as were formulated by the Fox Film Corporation in 1919 for one Charles (Buck) Gebhart, who was being elevated from the ranks of stunt men. Fox executives renamed him Buck Jones and issued the following instructions:

Please give painstaking attention to the following:
   1) Your hair must always be neatly combed unless you are in a fight. Have it cut, washed and oiled once a week to give it proper gloss.
   2) Your teeth require polishing and cleaning by a dentist once every two months and careful attention daily. Open your mouth a little wider when you smile so that your teeth are seen more.
   3) The new suits of clothes, shirts and collars you are having made should be worn so that you will get in practice of wearing those kind of clothes and will not appear strange in them before the camera.
   4) You should give attention to your fingernails so they are clipped not too close and are always clean.

The cowboy's morals received similar attention. Gene Autry, with the approval of the industry, issued his colleagues a set of commandments that, had they been

---

HEAVY FINGERS ON WESTERN TRIGGERS

Some were well-groomed and oily smooth, others unshaven and mean of temper. Either way, villains were as essential to Western films as heroes. Though only a few film buffs knew their names, the faces of several actors who played "heavies" in movie after movie became familiar to a worldwide audience. Each had expertise in a particular role, though some, like Harry Woods, were equally convincing as head of an outlaw band or as one of the gang. Trevor Bardette was most at home leading a lynch mob. Noah Beery Sr. specialized in chicanery under a gloss of respectability, while Richard Cramer's intimidating bulk typecast him as the rough, heavy-handed heavy.

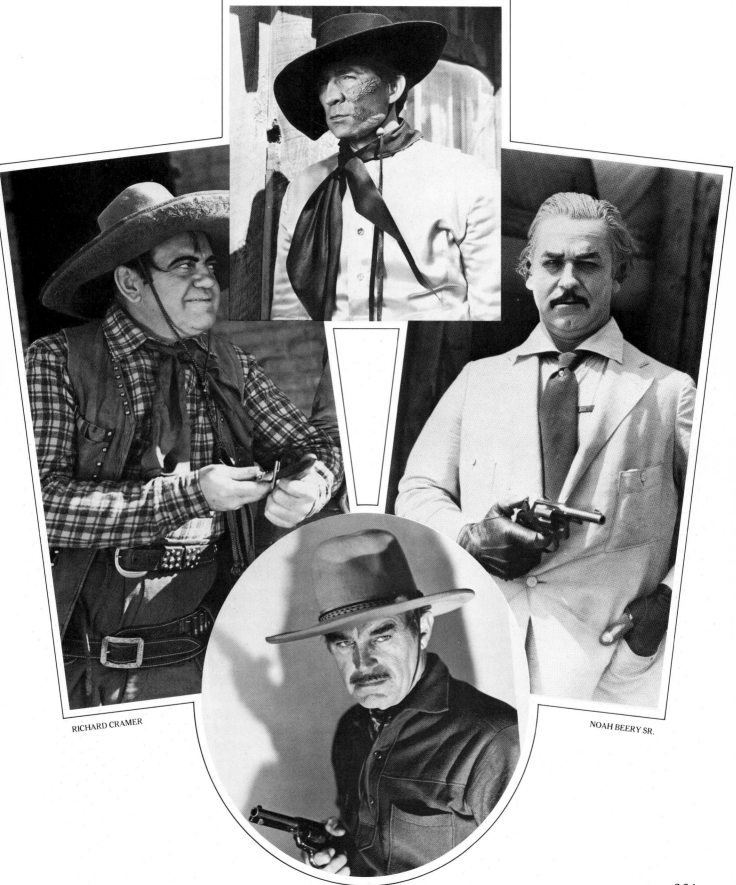

TREVOR BARDETTE

RICHARD CRAMER

NOAH BEERY SR.

HARRY WOODS

enforced on the old frontier, would have stopped westward expansion at the Mississippi. The cowboy, by these mandates, did not take unfair advantage of an enemy, never went back on his word, always told the truth, lifted neither voice nor hand to children, old folks or animals, hated intolerance of a racial or religious nature, helped all in distress, worked hard, respected women, parenthood and the law, was pure in thought, word and deed, did not smoke or drink and was true, in all circumstances, to the Red, White and Blue.

But Mix and his imitators—even while leading the Western off into the box canyons of showbiz—abided by certain philosophical absolutes that had been observed by Ince, Griffith, Broncho Billy and William S. Hart himself. Their horse operas told audiences what Teddy Roosevelt had written and Frederick Jackson Turner had implied about the West and Westerners: that the land was awesome and its conquerors a superior race of men. It was no place for weakness or indecision. A Western hero, whether Gibson or Acord, Hart or Mix, did not moon about; he leaped on his trusty horse and ACTED. The message was one of hope: the cavalry would arrive in time.

The studios stuck to the basic tenets of this B-picture mythology even in their occasional serious (i.e. big-budget) Westerns, though they sometimes made a few concessions in the direction of realism since these epics, as they came to be called, were usually based on historical characters and events, or on well-known literary properties.

The term "epic" as applied to Westerns is said to have been coined in 1922 by Jesse Lasky, vice president of Paramount Pictures, as he was trying to justify spending the horrendous sum of $500,000 to film Emerson Hough's novel *The Covered Wagon*. The company's president, Adolph Zukor, telephoned Lasky from New York to ask him if he had not misplaced a decimal point in making out his quarterly budget. "No," said Lasky nervously, "it will cost half a million." Bill Hart's last picture, *Three Word Brand*, was doing badly, said Zukor. Westerns seemed to be going out of style. He was not inclined to invest so much money in one. "But this," said Lasky desperately, "is more than a Western. It is an epic." Silence fell. Lasky spelled the word. "An epic, eh?" said Zukor at last. "Well. That's different. Go ahead."

The Covered Wagon cost three quarters of a million, as things turned out—seven times the budget of an ordinary fast-action horse opera—but this first Western epic dramatized the triumphs and tribulations of westbound Americans on a scale audiences had never seen before.

Its director, James Cruze, scoured half the West before deciding on 200,000 acres in Nevada's Snake Valley as his location. He hired 1,000 extras, hundreds of technicians, a herd of buffalo and 750 Indians. He assigned eight big trucks to the task of bringing food and supplies to the tent city he erected to house laborers and cast. And he borrowed, leased or built 500 covered wagons—a caravan three miles long—and secured the animals needed to haul them across the rough terrain. His Hollywood pioneers found themselves coping with many of the hardships and difficulties that real pioneers had experienced 80 years before; their wagon train was beset by wind, dust, heat, high water and, at one point, a genuine blizzard, which was hastily written into the script.

Audiences were struck by the grandeur of the scenery and the scale of the action; *The Covered Wagon* was a tremendous success. It played at Grauman's Hollywood Egyptian Theater in Los Angeles for months and paid for itself with its earnings there and at just one other theater, the Criterion in New York. It prompted a revival in the then-declining Western genre and created a vogue in epics that lasted for several years. But the film itself, by general critical consensus, was of limited artistic value. Sweeping vistas notwithstanding, the picture focused on a routine love-triangle story and failed to convey the historical or personal significance of the trek across the mountains and plains. Many of the action sequences were clumsily staged and edited, moreover, and lacked the excitement that is the Western's stock in trade. The Western epic attained its full stature a year later, however—in the hands of a talented young veteran of dozens of assembly-line oaters, John Ford.

Ford, christened Sean O'Feeney, was born and grew up in Cape Elizabeth, Maine, the youngest child of immigrant parents, and was drawn to California as a young man because an older brother—who called himself Francis Ford—had found work there as an actor and director in silent films. Sean billed himself as Jack

Actor Johnny Mack Brown beats a slow-drawing villain to the trigger in the 1944 film, *Range Law.* The wounded bad guy's excruciated grimace as he drops his pistol was a hallmark of shoot-out scenes.

Ford to avoid confusing his brother's employers, and picked up odd jobs as a property man and, after a while, as a bit actor. Carl Laemmle, seeing him shift props at Universal, supposedly ordered: "He hollers the loudest. Make him a director." And a director he was, whether at Laemmle's behest or not, by the age of 21—a young man filled with force and ideas, cranking out Western two-reelers on the back lot at Universal and dealing with Hollywood's cowboy actors on their own terms.

Ford guided Hoot Gibson through some of the ex-rodeo star's early short films, and also shared an apartment with him, drank with him and, on one memorable occasion, broke a piano stool over his head. "He was worse Irish than me," remembered Gibson afterward. "He wanted to play 'My Wild Irish Rose' on the player piano and I wanted something else. He picked up the piano stool and broke it on my head. And it was my piano!" The incident did not diminish Gibson's admiration for the young director; he considered Ford to be "close to a genius," as would many another actor in years to come.

Ford proved himself before a wider audience and became one of Hollywood's leading film makers with *The Iron Horse,* an epic based on construction of the first transcontinental railroad and the Fox Film Corporation's answer to *The Covered Wagon.* Ford outdid Cruze in lavishing care and money on his films. Ford

223

John Ford *(right)* directs *The Iron Horse.* Ford admitted that his movies touched up the images of some of the real West's less virtuous figures, but he said, "It's good for the country to have heroes to look up to."

hired, according to studio publicists, 5,000 extras, including a complete regiment of U.S. Cavalry, 1,000 Chinese construction hands and 800 Indians. He installed 100 cooks to feed them all and had 2,800 horses, 1,300 buffalo and 10,000 head of cattle delivered to a section of Nevada desert on which the picture was filmed.

Ford, like Cruze, put his faith in a tried-and-true plot rather than in the sweep of history in striving for his audience's attention: his picture turned on the hero's efforts to revenge himself on his father's murderer, a white renegade who had become the leader of hostile Indians. But *The Iron Horse* gave movie audiences a sense of movement and action that *The Covered Wagon* had lacked and Ford added the intuitive touches—Indians seen dramatically on a skyline, a dog resting its head on a fallen warrior's body—that later became his trademarks. And although *The Covered Wagon* has a significant place in the history of Western movies, *The Iron Horse* has proved much more influential: dozens of imitators borrowed from it, and Cecil B. De Mille lifted whole sequences, some copied shot-for-shot, to make his own railroad epic, *Union Pacific,* years later.

Ford made another Western in 1926 and then abandoned the genre altogether for 13 years. But

Stagecoach, the film he made on his return, has come to be widely regarded as the standard against which all other Westerns must be measured. The story was scarcely original even in 1939; it recounts the trials of a disparate group of people traveling on a stagecoach under threat of Indian attack. The passengers are Hollywood's predictable representatives of virtue and villainy: the unjustly imprisoned fugitive bent on avenging his father's murder, the respectable but larcenous banker, the discreetly pregnant Southern gentlewoman, the chivalrous gambler, the nervous whiskey drummer, the alcoholic doctor, the comical driver and, of course, the noble whore. But these overworked stereotypes are so enlivened by Ford's vigorous treatment, and by the bravura of his cast, that their very triteness becomes an asset—a reaffirmation of the fundamentals of the Western myth.

And the picture is distinguished, quite apart from its melodrama, by one of the most spectacular chase sequences ever filmed and by the majesty of Monument Valley, Utah—which Ford used as a location for the first time in *Stagecoach* and was to reuse so often as to make it a central icon in the Western imagery of Hollywood. But *Stagecoach* may be best remembered as the film that rescued an actor named John Wayne from the nether world of B-pictures and in time made him—more than anyone since Tom Mix, more even than Gary Cooper—Hollywood's embodiment of the Western hero.

Wayne—true name, Marion Mitchell Morrison—was born in Iowa, the son of a small-town druggist, and grew up in California after his parents moved west. He picked up the nickname "Duke" from a part he was drafted to play in a high school melodrama. He abandoned the theater for football at the University of Southern California but got into the motion picture business in 1927 as a prop boy and occasional extra at the Fox Studios. He launched himself toward bigger things by his response to a curiously sadistic little incident that John Ford contrived while Wayne was being used as a football player in a picture entitled *Salute.* The director objected to the way Wayne was using the lineman's three-point stance and sent him chin first into the ground by kicking away his supporting arm. Wayne asked his tormentor for more specific guidance and then, as Ford bent over to demonstrate, kicked him into

a pool of mud. Ford laughed—winning Wayne's loyalty for life—and admitted him, shortly, to a circle of cronies with whom he played pitch between takes.

Young Marion Morrison was on his own, nevertheless, during the next decade. He got his screen name and his first big part from another director, Raoul Walsh, who cast him as the lead in *The Big Trail,* one of the first sound Westerns and an ambitious wagon-train epic on the order of *The Covered Wagon.* The film was a triumph of mud-soaked realism and mass action, but perhaps because audiences were uncomfortable with talking Westerns, or perhaps because of the wooden performance of the film's inexperienced leading man, *The Big Trail* flopped at the box office and John

Wayne was consigned to B-Westerns for years to come. Wayne was not content with his career on Poverty Row, but the rigors of grinding out 10 oaters a year enabled him to develop skills that were to serve him well in the future. He became the acolyte, friend and colleague of Enos "Yakima" Canutt, Hollywood's stunt man supreme.

Canutt, a rancher's son and a marvelous athlete, was one of the very greatest of broncobusters in a day before rodeo began making headlines, and had as much to do with the kinetics of the Western motion picture while working without credit later on as did many a leading actor and director. He was a star in silent Westerns, but in talkies like *The Kansas Terrors, Range De-*

225

Winning the west with songs from the saddle

It was, one film historian wrote later, "closer to Tin Pan Alley than the Great Divide." Wyatt Earp would surely have agreed. But Western B-movie fans loved it when "America's Singin'est Cowboy," Gene Autry *(right),* leisurely crooned a tune after saving a heroine or rounding up the bad guys. In the 1930s and 1940s, celluloid gunslingers packed more ammunition in their vocal cords than in the chambers of their six guns.

Though actor Ken Maynard became the screen's first musical cowpoke in the late 1920s, it was Autry, with his 1935 film serial *The Phantom Empire,* who ushered in Westerns in which any excuse for a song, related to the story or not, was good enough. By the time *The Singing Cowboy* appeared in 1936, Autry personified the title, and reports of his packed houses had already spawned a rash of imitators.

In 1935, Dick Foran joined the frontier yodelers in *Moonlight on the Prairie.* A year later, Fred Scott, "The Silvery-Voiced Baritone," trolled his way to Western stardom in *Romance Rides the Range,* and Tex Ritter debuted in *Song of the Gringo.* By 1938, when Roy Rogers' first big feature, *Under Western Stars,* was released, gun-toting crooners were almost as plentiful as their unmusical forerunners.

The era of the singing cowboy began coming to a close in the late 1940s as Americans abandoned movie houses to watch old Westerns on television. Rogers, probably the only cowboy warbler to rival Autry's appeal, starred in his last lyrical oater in 1952. However, Hollywood had created an alluring mythology: the West where a cowboy's most compelling tune once echoed from a six gun had become a region where anything could be had for a song.

Singing cowboy Gene Autry strums a tune while sitting astride his horse, Champion.

fenders, The Dawn Rider and *Fighting Through* he was usually cast as the villain, often doubling for the hero in stunt scenes during the same picture. He put his mark on bigger films over the years by exercising something close to genius as a stunt man and, eventually, as a second-unit director contriving and superintending hair-raising action sequences involving crews of stunt men and often scores of extras.

His most celebrated stunt was a masterpiece of precisely choreographed daredeviltry. Canutt (while doubling for the hero) spurred his horse after a fleeing stagecoach, leaped from the saddle and grabbed the rear end of the vehicle, scrambled atop it, fought the villain, was knocked forward and fell between the galloping wheel horses, clung briefly to the wooden wagon tongue, let go, grabbed the rear axle as it passed over him, hauled himself upward after being dragged wildly along the ground, and—emerging once more on the roof of the coach—disposed of the startled villain for good.

Wayne met Canutt when Monogram Pictures hired the ex-broncobuster as his double (at considerably more money than Wayne was receiving) for a series of B-Westerns in which Wayne was playing the leading roles. The two men drank together around nighttime campfires on location and took to each other. The stunt man taught Wayne how to handle horses, which he had approached, theretofore, with real misgivings. The young actor modeled himself after Canutt, particularly by aping the ex-cowboy's way of walking, making it an integral part of his performances. And when Wayne was admitted to the big time in *Stagecoach,* he brought Canutt with him as stunt man and second-unit director in order to lend his magic to the film's climactic chase scene.

Wayne himself had become resigned to playing out his career on Poverty Row when John Ford offered him the part that was to make him a major star. The director broke the news with diabolic indirection. He took Wayne for a cruise on his yacht, *Araner,* showed him the 123-page script of *Stagecoach,* asked his advice in casting the part of the hero, the Ringo Kid, and then snorted with disgust when his hapless passenger suggested Lloyd Nolan. Wayne drank himself to sleep and was subjected, the next day, to persistent jibes about his stagnant career. He had a massive hangover when the boat docked at San Pedro. "Duke,"

said Ford, surveying him with satisfaction, "I want you to play the Ringo Kid."

The director withstood the urging of his financial backers to use Gary Cooper for the part, though he was risking his reputation with his first sound Western. Yet when filming began, he continued to harass Wayne. "Goddamn fairy," he said at one point. "Put your feet down like you were a man." He exacted a fine performance from his ex-prop boy as it turned out, and they entered into a master-pupil relationship that went on for decades. Wayne became one of a small circle of hulking actors with whom Ford liked to drink and play cards; he called the director "coach" and would leave a dinner party in minutes if summoned to the great man's house across town.

This curious friendship prompted a distinguished series of Westerns; Ford broke with convention by casting his admirer, who was by now approaching middle age, as a sardonic cavalry officer, a testy loner, a stern patriarch, and Wayne, in responding, became the biggest and one of the most enduring stars of motion pictures. Wayne was eventually granted strict control over his films, but regularly shaped his roles to the concepts of his mentor. He played 19th Century men with utter conviction during 30 long years as one of the greatest box-office attractions of Hollywood—and became such an institution in doing so that he seemed to be a figure of history and not a creature of electronic fiction at all.

And indeed, John Wayne did make history, as did Tom Mix and Bill Hart and hundreds of other Hollywood cowboys, and William Cody and Ned Buntline and Teddy Roosevelt and Frederic Remington and Dad Joiner and Casey Tibbs and even, for that matter, Five Minutes to Midnight. The myths they wove and those woven about them were in themselves a force that shaped the history of the West and of the country as a whole. These idealized visions of the Old West bore little relation, in many cases, to the real lives of the cowboys, ranchers, soldiers, miners and settlers who populated the region; but seldom, even at their most extreme, did the myths violate the hopes of those who had crossed the plains—or of the people who have since been affected in a thousand different ways by remembering them. Nations, too, must dream.

227

RAIL ROAD
CROSSING
3
TRACKS
MOST INTERESTIN
T in THE OLD WEST
VISIT • WATCH
WHERE REAL INDIA
DE
as featured in LIFE • New Mexico • LO
es & Newspapers all over U.S.
COME IN
AND BROWSE
No Oblig on

Hard sell among ghosts of the past

The trappings of commercial civilization have replaced the Old West of pioneers, quick-handed gunfighters and defiant Indian chieftains. Many of the cattle towns and mining camps have become modern cities, their skylines of office and apartment towers indistinguishable from those of the East. Automobiles whiz across the prairies on eight-lane highways built over the same trails that once carried bawling cattle or plodding wagon trains.

For all the changes, there are still lingering remnants of the past, for those who care to look for them. There are places where ranchers continue to graze their stock on seemingly boundless grasslands. Long-abandoned ghost towns tell of a time when the West was young and lusty. And the grandeur of the land, much of it unchanged and unchangeable, remains — although frequently as a backdrop to the encroachments of a modern age.

Some of the roadside enterprises that cater to the Western tourist trade seem to make a travesty of the men and women of all races who lived and died on the nation's frontier. But even this is a part of the Western heritage: entrepreneurs have distorted and exploited the West's romantic reputation ever since the first Eastern dude stepped off a train and went looking for the dime-novel frontier. The durable symbols of that version of the Old West live on.

Gas pumps and a coin-operated bronco stand in front of this New Mexico trading post. The products inside were made by local Indians.

At the establishment opposite, cut into a mountain near Moab, Utah, tourists can buy Indian trinkets and view "famous art and taxidermy." The carved head at the lower right is meant to portray President Franklin D. Roosevelt.

The motel cabins above, in Holbrook, Arizona, are shaped like wigwams, although the Apaches who once ranged nearby (some were transported from Holbrook to exile in Florida in 1886) lived in dome-shaped wickiups.

Traffic rumbles across a bridge from Mexico to El Paso, Texas, shimmering in the soft light of a 1970s desert sunset. Once a rip-roaring cattle town, El Paso is now a large modern city where tourism is a leading industry.

The sources for the illustrations in this book are shown below. Credits from left to right are separated by semicolons and from top to bottom by dashes.

Cover: Courtesy Don Look, Boulder, Colorado. 2: Courtesy Wyoming State Museum. 6, 7: Courtesy Buffalo Bill Historical Center, Cody, Wyoming. 8, 9: Courtesy Colorado Historical Society. 10, 11: Courtesy Title Insurance and Trust Collection, San Diego Historical Society. 12, 13: Courtesy Buffalo Bill Historical Center, Cody, Wyoming. 14: Courtesy Fern Kelly, Monitor, Washington. 16, 17: Courtesy Mrs. James O'Hara, Fielder Collection, Devereaux Library, South Dakota School of Mines & Technology, Rapid City, South Dakota. 18: Courtesy Beinecke Rare Book and Manuscript Library, Yale University (3), except top right: Courtesy George V. Allen Collection. 20: Courtesy The Society of California Pioneers. 21: Courtesy Denver Public Library, Western History Department. 22: Courtesy Library of Congress. 24: Courtesy Douglas County Museum—Leo Touchet, courtesy San Antonio Museum Association, Witte Memorial Museum, San Antonio, Texas. 25: Benschneider, from the collections of the Oklahoma Historical Society (2); Leo Touchet, courtesy San Antonio Museum Association, Witte Memorial Museum, San Antonio, Texas. 26: Courtesy The Huntington Library, San Marino, California. 28, 29: Courtesy Title Insurance and Trust Collection, San Diego Historical Society. 30, 31: Courtesy California Historical Society. 33: Courtesy Nebraska State Historical Society. 36, 37: Courtesy South Dakota State Historical Society. 38, 39: Courtesy Sumner W. Matteson Collection, Milwaukee Public Museum. 40, 41: Courtesy Denver Public Library, Western History Department. 42, 43: Courtesy History Division, Los Angeles County Museum of Natural History. 44, 45: Courtesy Buffalo Bill Historical Center, Cody, Wyoming. 46, 47: Courtesy The Hoblitzelle Theatre Arts Library, Humanities Research Center, the University of Texas at Austin. 48: Courtesy Denver Public Library, Western History Department. 49: Courtesy Circus World Museum, Baraboo, Wisconsin. 50, 51: Courtesy Theatre Collection, The New York Public Library at Lincoln Center, Astor, Lenox and Tilden Foundations. 52: Benschneider, courtesy Buffalo Bill Historical Center, Cody, Wyoming. 54: Courtesy Library of Congress. 55, 56: Benschneider, courtesy Buffalo Bill Historical Center, Cody, Wyoming. 57: Benschneider, courtesy Buffalo Bill's Memorial Museum, Lookout Mountain, Colorado. 58: Courtesy Wyoming State Museum. 59: Courtesy Denver Public Library, Western History Department. 60, 61: Courtesy Wyoming State Museum. 63: Courtesy Ringling Museum of the Circus, Sarasota, Florida. 65: Courtesy Denver Public Library, Western History Department (2). 67: Courtesy Denver Public Library, Western History Department. 68: Steven Mays, courtesy Collection of Jean E. Zerries. 69: Courtesy Library of Congress (2), except top right, courtesy The Huntington Library, San Marino, California. 70: Benschneider, from the Collection of Dick and Kathy Ralston; Benschneider, courtesy Ray Falconer. 71: Benschneider, from the Collection of Dick and Kathy Ralston (3). 72, 73: Courtesy *The Illustrated London News;* courtesy Biblioteca Nazionale Centrale-Rome. 74, 75: Courtesy Denver Public Library, Western History Department. 77: Courtesy Circus World Museum, Baraboo, Wisconsin. 78, 79: Courtesy Interfoto-Friedrich Rauch, courtesy Kurt Ulrich, Munich (2). 80, 81: Courtesy Kurt Ulrich, Munich; courtesy Interfoto-Friedrich Rauch, courtesy Kurt Ulrich, Munich. 82: Benschneider, courtesy Buffalo Bill's Memorial Museum, Lookout Mountain, Colorado. 83: Courtesy Darien House Inc. 84: Courtesy Theatre Collection, The New York Public Library at Lincoln Center, Astor, Lenox and Tilden Foundations. 86, 87: Courtesy Library of Congress. 88, 89: Courtesy Western History Collections, University of Oklaho-

ma. 90, 91: Courtesy Dr. J. S. Palen, Cheyenne, Wyoming. 92, 93: Courtesy Wyoming State Museum. 94 through 97: Courtesy The Encino Press and the University of Texas at Permian Basin. 98, 99: Benschneider, picture given by the Irwin Family. 100, 101: Courtesy Wyoming State Museum. 102: Courtesy Howdyshell Collection, Pendleton, Oregon. 103: Courtesy Wyoming State Museum—courtesy University of Wyoming Western History Research Center. 104: Courtesy Mr. and Mrs. J. C. (Chester) Kirkpatrick. 105: Courtesy Oregon Historical Society. 106, 107: Courtesy Goldbeck Collection, Humanities Research Center, the University of Texas at Austin. 109: From George Norman's Black Odyssey History and Art Exhibit. 110, 111: Courtesy Wyoming State Museum. 112: Courtesy Wyoming State Museum—Courtesy Dr. J. S. Palen, Cheyenne, Wyoming. 113: Frank Griggs, Bartlesville, Oklahoma—courtesy Wyoming State Museum. 115: Courtesy Juanita Gray—courtesy Smithers Collection, Humanities Research Center, the University of Texas at Austin. 117: Al Freni; N. R. Farbman for LIFE. 118, 119: Courtesy Wyoming State Museum. 121: Courtesy Jim Krieg, Billings, Montana. 122, 123: Courtesy Denver Public Library, Western History Department. 124: Henry Groskinsky, courtesy The Seamen's Bank for Savings. 127: Benschneider, courtesy The Rockwell-Corning Museum, Corning, New York. 128: Courtesy Theodore Roosevelt Collection, Harvard College Library. 129: Courtesy Library of Congress. 130: Courtesy Theodore Roosevelt Collection, Harvard College Library. 133: Gerald R. Brimacombe, courtesy National Park Service, Theodore Roosevelt National Memorial Park—Al Freni, courtesy Mrs. Robert T. Gannett (2). 134, 135: Henry Groskinsky, courtesy National Park Service, Sagamore Hill National Historic Site. 136: Al Freni, courtesy Mr. and Mrs. Herbert J. Siegel, Wyncote, Pennsylvania. 138, 139: Courtesy Theodore Roosevelt Collection, Harvard College Library. 143: Courtesy Library of Congress. 144, 145: Courtesy Remington Art Museum, Ogdensburg, New York. All rights reserved. 146, 147: Courtesy Theodore Roosevelt Collection, Harvard College Library. 148, 149: Courtesy Library of Congress (4). 150: Underwood & Underwood. 153: Courtesy Photographic Collection, American Museum of Natural History Library, New York. 154, 155: Ellis Herwig, courtesy The Museum of Fine Arts, Boston. 156, 157: John Blaustein, courtesy the E. B. Crocker Art Gallery, Sacramento, California. 158, 159: Courtesy the National Collection of Fine Arts, Smithsonian Institution; lent by the U.S. Department of the Interior. 160, 161: Benschneider, courtesy Oklahoma Historical Society. 162: Courtesy The Spindletop Museum of Lamar University. 164: Courtesy American Petroleum Institute Historical Photographs. 165: Leo Touchet, courtesy The Spindletop Museum of Lamar University. 166: Leo Touchet, donated to the Tyrrell Historical Library, Beaumont, Texas, by the George W. Carroll Family. 168, 169: Courtesy Fred A. Schell and American Petroleum Institute Historical Photographs. 170: From library files of the *Wichita Falls Times,* photo by Voyle N. Armstrong. 171: Leo Touchet, courtesy The Spindletop Museum of Lamar University. 173: Courtesy William Deming Hornaday Collection, Texas State Archives—courtesy The Barker Texas History Center, the University of Texas at Austin. 174, 175: Courtesy University of Louisville Photographic Archives, Standard Oil Collection. 176: Courtesy David R. Phillips Collection. 178, 179: Courtesy Library of Congress; courtesy The Permian Basin Petroleum Museum, Library and Hall of Fame, Midland, Texas. 180, 181: Courtesy Phillips Petroleum Company, except inset, reproduction of *Tulsa Daily World* front page—courtesy Oklahoma Archives Association. 184: Courtesy Cities Service Company Historical File, photo by Frank Griggs. 185: Courtesy University of Wyoming Western History Research Center. 186, 187: Courtesy University of Louisville Photographic Archives, Standard Oil Collection. 188, 189: Courtesy Phillips Petroleum Company (2). 190: Leo Touchet, courtesy The Spindletop Museum of Lamar University. 192, 193: Courtesy Marc Wanamaker, Bison Archives. 194, 195: Courtesy William Everson. 196, 197: Courtesy Academy of Motion Picture Arts & Sciences. 198, 199: Courtesy Collection of the International Museum of Photography at Rochester, New York. 200: Courtesy Academy of Motion Picture Arts & Sciences. 202, 203: Courtesy Culver Pictures (2). 204, 205: © Norman Alley Cody Collection (3). 208, 209: Courtesy Culver Pictures. 210: Courtesy Collection of International Museum of Photography at Rochester, New York (2). 211: Courtesy Culver Pictures. 213: Courtesy Academy of Motion Picture Arts & Sciences—courtesy Collection of the International Museum of Photography at Rochester, New York—courtesy William Everson. 214: Courtesy Kobal Collection, London. 215: Courtesy William Everson. 216: Courtesy The Janus Barfoed Collection, Denmark. 218: Marc Wanamaker, Bison Archives. 219: From the Collection of Alan G. Barbour; anonymous—courtesy Academy of Motion Picture Arts & Sciences. 221: Clockwise—from the Collection of Alan G. Barbour—courtesy The Museum of Modern Art/Film Stills Archive/NYC—courtesy William Everson (2). 223: Courtesy William Everson. 224: Courtesy Octopus Books, London. 225: Courtesy Academy of Motion Picture Arts & Sciences. 226: Courtesy Gene Autry. 228 through 233: Richard Ansaldi.

ACKNOWLEDGMENTS

The index for this book was prepared by Gale Partoyan. The editors give special thanks to Charles Angermeyer, Director, Denver Film Society, Colorado; Richard Etulain, Professor of History, Idaho State University, Pocatello; William Everson, Professor of Film, New York University; Walter Rundell, Professor of History, University of Maryland, College Park; G. Edward White, School of Law, University of Virginia, Charlottesville; and George Williams, Rodeo Historical Society, Cowboy Hall of Fame, Oklahoma City, who read and commented on the text. The editors also thank: George B. Abdill, Douglas County Museum, Roseburg, Oregon; David Allen, Rodeo News Bureau, Denver; David Anthony, W. H. Crain, Ed Neal, Hoblitzelle Theatre Collection, the University of Texas at Austin; Shelley Arlen, John Ezell, Jack Haley, Emily Myers, Western History Collections, University of Oklahoma, Norman; Mark Behler, North Central Washington Museum, Wenatchee; Ray Allen Billington, Alan Jutzi, Martin Ridge, Huntington Library, San Marino, California; John Carter, Wendell Frantz, Nebraska State Historical Society, Lincoln; John D. Cleaver, Steve Tanasoca, Janice Worden, Oregon Historical Society, Portland; Reba Collins, Will Rogers Memorial, Claremore, Oklahoma; Mel Crader, Jim Fitchette, Mary Jane Norfleet, Phillips Petroleum Co., Bartlesville, Oklahoma; Wilbur Cross, Continental Oil Co., Stamford, Connecticut; David Crosson, Western History Research Center, University of Wyoming, Laramie; Wallace Finley Dailey, Theodore Roosevelt Collection, Harvard College Library, Cambridge, Massachusetts; Lori Davisson, Arizona Historical Society, Tucson; Tony Dean, Linda Young, Yellowstone National Park Library and Museum, Wyoming; Carl S. Dentzel, Southwest Museum, Los Angeles, California; Richard Drew, American Petroleum Institute, Washington, D.C.; James Ebert, Theodore Roosevelt Birthplace, New York, New York; Ray Falconer, Ponca City, Oklahoma; Bill Fannin, Calvin Smith, Spindletop Museum, Lamar University, Beaumont, Texas; Paula Fleming, James Gregg, National Anthropological Archives, Smithsonian Institution, Washington, D.C.; Homer Fort, Betty Orbeck, Permian Basin Petroleum Museum, Midland, Texas; Lee Frigeau, Elizabeth, Colorado; Richard Frost, Peter Hassrick, Sheri Hoem, Leo Platteter, Buffalo Bill Historical Center, Cody, Wyoming; John Gable, Theodore Roosevelt Association, Oyster Bay, New York; Sam Garrett, Garrett Ranch, Fallbrook, California; Dick and Connie Griffiths, Wickenburg, Arizona; Frank N. Griggs, Bartlesville, Oklahoma; Archibald Hanna, Beinecke Library, Yale University, New Haven, Connecticut; William Herr, Theodore Roosevelt National Memorial Park, Medora, North Dakota; Chuck Hornung, Lubbock, Texas; Mel Houghton, "Stonefield," Cassville, Wisconsin; John Hurdle, Ringling Circus Museum, Sarasota, Florida; Matt Johnson, Howdyshell Photos, Pendleton, Oregon; Michael Kamins, International Museum of Photography, Rochester, New York; Jerry Kearns, Library of Congress, Washington, D.C.; Fern Kelly, Monitor, Washington; Mr. and Mrs. J. Chester Kirkpatrick, Pendleton, Oregon; Richard P. LaGuardia, Buffalo Bill Memorial Museum, Golden, Colorado; Bonita Lang, Council Bluffs, Iowa; Mary Ellen MacNamara, Humanities Research Center, the University of Texas at Austin; Martha R. Mahard, Harvard Theatre Collection, Pusey Library, Cambridge, Massachusetts; Marty Martins, Rodeo News, Pauls Valley, Oklahoma; A. D. Mastrogiuseppe, Denver Public Library, Colorado; Patricia McDonough, Rochester Museum and Science Center, New York; John McKern, Ann Arbor, Michigan; Annabelle Monnet, Tulsa County Historical Museum, Oklahoma; Marjorie Morey, Amon Carter Museum, Fort Worth, Texas; Pat Morris, Wenatchee, Washington; Elizabeth Moyer, Gretchen Worden, Mutter Museum, Philadelphia, Pennsylvania; George Norman, Detroit, Michigan; Debbie Olander, Parker Brothers, Salem, Massachusetts; Greg and Robert Parkinson, Circus World Museum, Baraboo, Wisconsin; Fred Phening, Columbus, Ohio; David R. Phillips, Chicago, Illinois; Tom Polansky, Santa Barbara, California; Mr. and Mrs. Richard Ralston, Boulder, Colorado; Gary Roth, Sagamore Hill National Historic Site, Oyster Bay, New York; Martin Schmitt, Brodie Washburn, University of Oregon Library, Eugene; Wendy Shadwell, New-York Historical Society, New York, New York; Pat Simmons, Bureau of Indian Affairs, Washington, D.C.; Annette Slahor, Raymond E. Utt, Cities Service Co., Tulsa, Oklahoma; Glenn Sonnedecker, University of Wisconsin, Madison; Betty Steele, Littleton, Colorado; Cecilia Steinfeldt, Witte Memorial Museum, San Antonio, Texas; Linda Stone, Woolaroc Museum, Bartlesville, Oklahoma; Jack Underwood, Publishing Industries, Inc., Oklahoma City, Oklahoma; Dan Walters, Wenatchee Public Library, Washington; Paula West, Wyoming State Archives, Cheyenne; Edgar E. Weston, Copan, Oklahoma; Bill Wittliff, Encino Press, Austin, Texas; Joyce Wright, Laramie Plains Museum, Wyoming; James Harvey Young, Emory University, Atlanta, Georgia.

Chapter I: Particularly useful sources for information and quotes in this chapter: Ray A. Billington, *America's Frontier Heritage,* Holt, Rinehart and Winston, 1966; Ray A. Billington, *Frederick Jackson Turner,* Oxford University Press, 1973; Edmund Pearson, *Dime Novels,* Little, Brown and Co., 1929; Frank R. Prassel, *The Western Peace Officer,* University of Oklahoma Press, 1972. Chapter II: John Burke, *Buffalo Bill, the Noblest Whiteskin,* G. P. Putnam's Sons, 1973; Don Russell, *The Lives and Legends of Buffalo Bill,* University of Oklahoma Press, 1973; Richard J. Walsh, *The Making of Buffalo Bill,* The Bobbs-Merrill Co., 1928. Chapter III: Foghorn Clancy, *My Fifty Years in Rodeo,* The Naylor Co., 1952; Robert D. Hanesworth, *Daddy of 'Em All: The Story of Cheyenne Frontier Days,* Flintlock Pub. Co., 1967; LIFE, "Champ Rider, Casey Tibbs," October 22, 1951; Clifford P. Westermeier, *Man, Beast, Dust: The Story of Rodeo,* Clifford P. Westermeier, 1947. Chapter IV: Charles H. Brown, *The Correspondent's War,* Charles Scribner's Sons, 1967; Hermann Hagedorn, *The Theodore Roosevelt Treasury,* G. P. Putnam's Sons, 1957; William H. Harbaugh, *The Life and Times of Theodore Roosevelt,* Oxford University Press, 1975; Elting Morison, editor, *The Letters of Theodore Roosevelt,* Harvard University Press, 1951; Theodore Roosevelt, *An Autobiography,* The Macmillan Co., 1913; Theodore Roosevelt, "The Rough Riders," Volume XI; "The Winning of the West," Volumes VIII, IX, *The Works of Theodore Roosevelt,* Charles Scribner's Sons, 1926; G. Edward White, *The Eastern Establishment and the Western Experience,* Yale University Press, 1968; Jack Willis, *Roosevelt in the Rough,* Ives Washburn, 1931. Chapter V: Mody C. Boatright, *Folklore of the Oil Industry,* Southern Methodist University Press, 1963; Mody C. Boatright and William A. Owens, *Tales from the Derrick Floor,* Doubleday & Co., Inc., 1970; Ruth S. Knowles, *The Greatest Gamblers: The Epic of American Oil Exploration,* McGraw-Hill Book Co., Inc., 1959. Chapter VI: William K. Everson, *History of the Western Film,* The Citadel Press, 1969; George N. Fenin and William K. Everson, *The Western from Silents to the Seventies,* Penguin Books, 1977; Jon Tuska, *The Filming of the West,* Doubleday & Co., Inc., 1976.

BIBLIOGRAPHY

Adams, Ramon F., *Prose and Poetry of the Live Stock Industry.* Antiquarian Press, Ltd., 1959.

Admari, Ralph, "The House that Beadle Built, 1859-1869," *The American Book Collector,* November 1933-February 1934.

Andrews, Wayne, ed., *The Autobiography of Theodore Roosevelt.* Octagon Books, 1975.

Ball, Max W., *This Fascinating Oil Business.* The Bobbs-Merrill Co., 1940.

Barbour, Alan G., *The Thrill of It All.* Collier Books, 1971.

Beitz, Les, "Heyday of the Pulp Westerns," *True West Magazine,* February 1967.

Billington, Ray A.:
America's Frontier Heritage. Holt, Rinehart and Winston, 1966.
Frederick Jackson Turner. Oxford Univ. Press, 1973.
Westward Expansion. The Macmillan Co., 1967.

Boatright, Mody C.:
Folklore of the Oil Industry. Southern Methodist Univ. Press, 1963.
and William A. Owens, *Tales from the Derrick Floor.* Doubleday & Co., Inc., 1970.

Bronson, William, *The Earth Shook, the Sky Burned.* Doubleday & Co., Inc., 1959.

Brown, Charles H., *The Correspondents' War.* Charles Scribner's Sons, 1967.

Brownlow, Kevin, *The Parade's Gone By.* Univ. of California Press, 1968.

Burke, John, *Buffalo Bill, the Noblest Whiteskin.* G. P. Putnam's Sons, 1973.

Burroughs, John, *Camping & Tramping with Roosevelt.* Houghton Mifflin Co., 1907.

Burton, David H.:
"The Influence of the American West on the Imperialist Philosophy of Theodore Roosevelt," *Arizona and the West,* Vol. 4, No. 1, Spring 1962.
Theodore Roosevelt. Twayne Publishers, Inc., 1972.

Cary, Diana S., *The Hollywood Posse.* Houghton Mifflin Co., 1975.

Clancy, Foghorn, *My Fifty Years in Rodeo.* The Naylor Co., 1952.

Clark, James A. and Michel T. Halbouty, *Spindletop.* Random House, 1952.

Collings, Ellsworth and Alma M. England, *The 101 Ranch.* Univ. of Oklahoma Press, 1971.

Davidson, Harold, *Edward Borein, Cowboy Artist.* Doubleday & Co., Inc., 1973.

Dolson, Hildegarde, *The Great Oildorado.* Random House, 1959.

Durham, Philip and Everett L. Jones, *The Negro Cowboys.* Dodd, Mead & Co., 1965.

Etulain, Richard W. and Michael Marsden, eds., "The Popular Western," *Journal of Popular Culture,* Vol. 7, No. 3.

Everson, William K., *History of the Western Film.* The Citadel Press, 1969.

Eyles, Allen, *The Western.* A. S. Barnes and Co., 1975.

Fenin, George N. and William K. Everson, *The Western from Silents to the Seventies.* Penguin Books, 1977.

Frantz, Joe B. and Julian E. Choate, Jr., *The American Cowboy: The Myth and the Reality.* Univ. of Oklahoma Press, 1955.

Frazer, Robert W., *Forts of the West.* Univ. of Oklahoma Press, 1965.

Freidel, Frank, *The Splendid Little War.* Bramhall House, 1958.

Friar, Ralph and Natasha, *The Only Good Indian.* Drama Book Specialists, 1972.

Furlong, Charles W.:
Let 'Er Buck. Singing Tree Press, 1971.
"Let 'Er Buck," *The World's Work,* February 1914.

Gregory, Robert, *Oil in Oklahoma.* Leake Industries, Inc., 1976.

Grey, Zane, *Riders of the Purple Sage.* Walter J. Black, Inc., 1940.

Hagedorn, Hermann, *The Theodore Roosevelt Treasury.* G. P. Putnam's Sons, 1957.

Hall, Douglas K., *Rodeo.* Ballantine Books, 1976.

Hanes, Bailey C., *Bill Pickett, Bulldogger.* Univ. of Oklahoma Press, 1977.

Hanesworth, Robert D., *Daddy of 'Em All: The Story of Cheyenne Frontier Days*. Flintlock Pub. Co., 1967.

Harbaugh, William H., *The Life and Times of Theodore Roosevelt*. Oxford Univ. Press, 1975.

Hart, Albert B. and Herbert R. Ferleger, *Theodore Roosevelt Cyclopedia*. Roosevelt Memorial Association, 1941.

House, Boyce, *Were You in Ranger?* Tardy Pub. Co., 1935.

Hunt, Frazier and Robert, *Horses and Heroes: The Story of the Horse in America for 450 Years*. Charles Scribner's Sons, 1949.

Jackson, Carlton, *Zane Grey*. Twayne Publishers, Inc., 1973.

Jacobs, Wilbur R., *Frederick Jackson Turner's Legacy*. Univ. of Nebraska Press, 1965.

Johannsen, Albert, *The House of Beadle and Adams*, Vols. I, II. Univ. of Oklahoma Press, 1950.

Jones, Daryl, *The Dime Novel Western*. Bowling Green Univ. Popular Press, 1978.

Knowles, Ruth S., *The Greatest Gamblers: The Epic of American Oil Exploration*. McGraw-Hill Book Co., Inc., 1959.

Lahue, Kalton C., *Winners of the West: The Sagebrush Heroes of the Silent Screen*. A. S. Barnes and Co., 1970.

Lamar, Howard R., *The Reader's Encyclopedia of the American West*. Thomas Y. Crowell Co., 1977.

Leithead, J. Edward, "25 Years of Glory," *True West Magazine*, February 1967.

LIFE, "Champ Rider, Casey Tibbs," October 22, 1951.

McClure, Arthur F. and Ken D. Jones, *Heroes, Heavies and Sagebrush: A Pictorial History of the "B" Western Players*. A. S. Barnes and Co., 1972.

Mathews, John J., *Life and Death of an Oilman: The Career of E. W. Marland*. Univ. of Oklahoma Press, 1951.

Miller, Don, *Hollywood Corral*. Popular Library, 1976.

Millis, Walter, *The Martial Spirit*. The Literary Guild, 1931.

Monaghan, Jay, *The Great Rascal: The Life and Adventures of Ned Buntline*. Bonanza Books, 1951.

Morison, Elting, ed., *The Letters of Theodore Roosevelt*. Harvard Univ. Press, 1951.

O'Connor, Richard, *The Oil Barons*. Little, Brown and Co., 1971.

Palen, J. S., "Cheyenne Frontier Days: Daddy of 'Em All," *Persimmon Hill*, Vol. 7, No. 3.

Pearson, Edmund, *Dime Novels*. Little, Brown and Co., 1929.

Place, J. A., *The Western Films of John Ford*. The Citadel Press, 1973.

Pomeroy, Earl:
In Search of the Golden West: The Tourist in Western America. Alfred A. Knopf, 1957.
The Pacific Slope. Alfred A. Knopf, 1965.

Prassel, Frank R., *The Western Peace Officer*. Univ. of Oklahoma Press, 1972.

Pringle, Henry F., *Theodore Roosevelt, a Biography*. Harcourt, Brace & World, Inc., 1956.

Reiger, John F., *American Sportsmen and the Origins of Conservation*. Winchester Press, 1975.

Remley, Mary L., "From Sidesaddle to Rodeo," *Journal of the West*, Vol. XVII, No. 3, July 1978.

Rister, Carl C., *Oil! Titan of the Southwest*. Univ. of Oklahoma Press, 1949.

Robertson, M. S., *Rodeo, Standard Guide to the Cowboy Sport*. Howell-North Books, 1961.

Rodeo News, Vol. 16, No. 12; Vol. 17, No. 1, December-January 1977.

Roosevelt, Theodore:
"American Problems," Vol. XVI; "The Rough Riders, Men of Action," Vol. XI; "The Winning of the West," Vols. VIII, IX; *The Works of Theodore Roosevelt*. Charles Scribner's Sons, 1926.
Theodore Roosevelt, an Autobiography. The Macmillan Co., 1913.
Theodore Roosevelt's Ranch Life and the Hunting Trail. Bonanza Books, 1915.

Rundell, Walter, Jr., *Early Texas Oil: A Photographic History, 1866-1936*. Texas A&M Univ. Press, 1977.

Russell, Don:
The Lives and Legends of Buffalo Bill. Univ. of Oklahoma Press, 1973.
The Wild West: A History of the Wild West Shows. Amon Carter Museum, 1970.

Smith, Henry N., *Virgin Land: The American West as Symbol and Myth*. Harvard Univ. Press, 1970.

Tait, Samuel W., Jr., *The Wildcatters: An Informal History of Oil Hunting in America*. Princeton Univ. Press, 1946.

Taylor, George R., ed., *The Turner Thesis*. D. C. Heath & Co., 1956.

Tiratsoo, E. N., *Oilfields of the World*. Scientific Press, Ltd., 1973.

Tuska, Jon, *The Filming of the West*. Doubleday & Co., Inc., 1976.

Tyler, Ron, *The Rodeo of John Addison Stryker*. The Encino Press, 1977.

Vidor, King, *A Tree is a Tree*. Garland Publishing, Inc., 1977.

Wagenknecht, Edward, *The Seven Worlds of Theodore Roosevelt*. Longmans, Green & Co., 1958.

Walsh, Richard J., *The Making of Buffalo Bill*. The Bobbs-Merrill Co., 1928.

Watkins, T. H., *California: An Illustrated History*. American West Pub. Co., 1973.

Watts, Peter, *A Dictionary of the Old West, 1850-1900*. Alfred A. Knopf, 1977.

Wayte, Harold C., Jr., "A History of Holbrook and the Little Colorado Country, 1840-1962" (unpublished dissertation, Univ. of Arizona, 1962).

Wecter, Dixon, *The Hero in America*. Univ. of Michigan Press, 1963.

Westermeier, Clifford P.:
Man, Beast, Dust: The Story of Rodeo. Clifford P. Westermeier, 1947.
The Western Range, Senate Document No. 199, April 24, 1936.

White, G. Edward, *The Eastern Establishment and the Western Experience*. Yale Univ. Press, 1968.

Williams, George, "C. B. Irwin: High Roller," *Persimmon Hill*, Vol. 7, No. 2.

Williamson, Harold F., Ralph L. Andreano, Arnold R. Daum, and Gilbert C. Klose, *The American Petroleum Industry*. Northwestern Univ. Press, 1963.

Willis, Jack, *Roosevelt in the Rough*. Ives Washburn, 1931.

Wilson, R. L., *Theodore Roosevelt: Outdoorsman*. Winchester Press, 1971.

Wister, Owen, *The Virginian*. Pocket Books, 1976.